BRITISH TROLLEYBUS SYSTEMS
WALES, MIDLANDS AND EAST ANGLIA

An Historic Overview

BRITISH TROLLEYBUS SYSTEMS
WALES, MIDLANDS AND EAST ANGLIA

An Historic Overview

PETER WALLER

AN IMPRINT OF PEN & SWORD BOOKS LTD.
YORKSHIRE – PHILADELPHIA

British Trolleybus Systems – Wales, Midlands and East Anglia

First published in Great Britain in 2023 by
Pen and Sword Transport
An imprint of
Pen & Sword Books Ltd.
Yorkshire - Philadelphia

Copyright © Peter Waller, 2023

ISBN 978 1 39902 248 4

The right of Peter Waller to be identified as Author of this work has been asserted by him in accordance with the Copyright, Designs and Patents Act 1988.

A CIP catalogue record for this book is available from the British Library.

All rights reserved. No part of this book may be reproduced or transmitted in any form or by any means, electronic or mechanical including photocopying, recording or by any information storage and retrieval system, without permission from the Publisher in writing.

Typeset in 11/13 Palatino by SJmagic DESIGN SERVICES, India.

Printed and bound by Printworks Global Ltd, London/Hong Kong.

Pen & Sword Books Ltd incorporates the Imprints of Pen & Sword Books Archaeology, Atlas, Aviation, Battleground, Discovery, Family History, History, Maritime, Military, Naval, Politics, Railways, Select, Transport, True Crime, Fiction, Frontline Books, Leo Cooper, Praetorian Press, Seaforth Publishing, Wharncliffe and White Owl.

For a complete list of Pen & Sword titles please contact

PEN & SWORD BOOKS LIMITED
47 Church Street, Barnsley, South Yorkshire, S70 2AS, England
E-mail: enquiries@pen-and-sword.co.uk
Website: www.pen-and-sword.co.uk

or

PEN AND SWORD BOOKS
1950 Lawrence Rd, Havertown, PA 19083, USA
E-mail: Uspen-and-sword@casematepublishers.com
Website: www.penandswordbooks.com

CONTENTS

Abbreviations 6
Acknowledgements 7
Introduction 8
Author's Note 11
Aberdare 12
Birmingham 16
Cardiff 26
Chesterfield 36
Derby 41
Grimsby-Cleethorpes 54
Ipswich 63
Llanelly 78
Nottingham 85
Notts & Derby 99
Pontypridd 105
Rhondda 111
Walsall 114
Wolverhampton 129
Bibliography 146

ABBREVIATIONS

ADC	Associated Daimler Co
AEC	Associated Equipment Co
BAMC	Blackburn Aeroplane & Motor Co Ltd
BCT	Bradford City Tramways
BET	British Electric Traction
BRCW	Birmingham Railway Carriage & Wagon Co Ltd
BTA	Bradford Trolleybus Association
BTH	British Thomson-Houston
BTS	British Trolleybus Society
BUT	British United Traction
Dodson	Christopher Dodson Ltd
EE	English Electric
EMB	Electro-Mechanical Brake Co Ltd
GEC	General Electric Co
GRCW	Gloucester Railway Carriage & Wagon Co Ltd
HN	Hurst Nelson
LCC	London County Council
LCT	Leeds City Tramways
LGOC	London General Omnibus Co
LMS	London, Midland & Scottish Railway
LRTL	Light Railway Transport League
LTHS	Leeds Transport Historical Society
LUT	London United Tramways
MCCW	Metropolitan-Cammell Carriage & Wagon Co Ltd
MET	Metropolitan Electric Tramways
MTMS	Manchester Transport Museum Society
NCB	Northern Coachbuilders Ltd
NTA	National Trolleybus Association
PR	Park Royal
RET	RET Construction Co Ltd
Roe	Charles H. Roe Ltd
RS&J	Ransomes, Sims & Jefferies
RTS	Reading Transport Society (later British Trolleybus Society)
South Met	South Metropolitan Electric Tramways & Lighting Co
TRTB	Teesside Railless Traction Board
UCC	United Construction & Finance Co
UDC	Urban District Council

ACKNOWLEDGEMENTS

This is one of four volumes that, between them, cover all of the trolleybus operators of the British Isles. The majority of the images used are drawn from the collection of the Online Transport Archive, which is a registered charity devoted to the preservation and conservation of images of primarily transport interest. Further information about the archive can be found at its website: www.onlinetransportarchive.org. I am grateful to the following for additional images and, in certain cases, for reading through and making comment on part or all of the manuscript: Colin Barker, Tony Fox, Dave Hall, Philip Kirk, Geoff Lumb, Mike Maybin and Hugh Taylor. It goes without saying that any errors are those of the author and please let him know via the publishers so that these can be corrected in any second or subsequent editions of the books.

INTRODUCTION

This is one of four volumes that will examine the history of all of the trolleybus operators in the British Isles. This one describes those operators based in Wales, Midlands and East Anglia.

Although the history of the trolleybus stretches back to early experiments in 1882 undertaken by Ernst Werner Siemens in Berlin it was not until the first decade of the twentieth century that interest in the British Isles was first to emerge. By this time the familiar system of parallel overhead wires with rigid trolleypoles, as pioneered by Max Schiemann in 1904, had come to dominate although there were other systems – such as the Cedes-Stoll, Lloyd-Kohler and Filovia – that also had their exponents and were to influence the development of a number of – short-lived – British systems. Before the introduction of trolleybuses to a number of British operators, delegations, particularly in the early days, travelled to Europe to see this new type of transport in operation.

Although Bradford and Leeds had the honour of opening Britain's first public trolleybus services in June 1911, there had been a number of experimental uses of the trolleybus prior to that date. An earlier generation of public transport – the tramway – had been established through a legislative framework following the Tramways Act of 1870 and much of the development of the trolleybus was also influenced by the law. The 1870 Act made the tramway operator responsible for the maintenance of the road surface stretching to a distance of eighteen inches outside the outer running rail on both sides and, for a period, there was a possibility that a similar cost burden might have been laid on trolleybus operators. This would undoubtedly have made most trolleybus installations prohibitively expensive and thus weakened the case for their introduction. Ironically, however, it was the state of these ill-maintained roads allied to the use of solid-tyred vehicles that represented the Achilles' heel for many of the early operators and led to many early casualties. Although the pneumatic tyre had been originally developed in the 1880s, it was not until the late 1920s that they were routinely fitted to trolleybuses.

When the trolleybus first appeared on Britain's streets there was no concept that it might replace the tram. The trolleybus represented a low-cost means of supplementing existing tram services on lightly trafficked routes and to provide links to communities that were not well served by existing services. There was also a belief that, in certain cases, the introduction of a trolleybus service would be a useful guide to potential traffic and thus be used as a precursor to the introduction of trams. The seating capacity of the new vehicles was severely limited – the first two vehicles in Bradford, for example, could accommodate twenty-eight seated passengers each – when a contemporary double-deck tram's capacity was double that. Moreover, fitted with conventional tramway controllers, trolleybuses were also cumbersome to drive.

It was the development of the first two fully-enclosed double-deck trolleybuses – Nos 521 and 522 – by Bradford Corporation in 1920 and 1922 that established, for the first time, the trolleybus as a serious competitor to the tram. For Britain's tramway operators, which had emerged from the First World War with a backlog of track and overhead maintenance allied to increasingly aged trams, the trolleybus seemed an ideal compromise for replacing the trams: they made use of much of the existing infrastructure – such as the output from the local power station – whilst were cheaper to operate and maintain. The pivotal point here was the decision in Birmingham to convert the Nechells tram route to trolleybus operation; when trolleybuses were introduced on 27 November 1922, this was the first service where trams had been supplanted. Over the succeeding months, a number of delegations visited Birmingham to see the Nechells route in operation and many of these subsequently adopted the trolleybus.

Although a significant number of operators looked at the possibility of introducing trolleybuses, the actual number of operators that made the trolleybus their primary means of public transport was limited. In his, ultimately futile, attempt to dissuade Cardiff Corporation from adopting the trolleybus, William Forbes the general manager came up with some telling statistics in the mid-1930s. He noted that seventy-four tramway systems had been abandoned between September 1931 and September 1937; of these, only eleven had adopted the trolleybus. Moreover, ten trolleybus systems had been converted to motorbus in the period since 1925. The adoption by the London Passenger Transport Board of the trolleybus for its tramway conversion programme was perhaps crucial in maintaining the viability of the trolleybus as a commercially attractive replacement (just as a generation later, the decision to phase the trolleybus out of service in the Metropolis probably sounded its death-knell).

The role of the individual cannot be overstated in the development of the trolleybus. Bradford was fortunate in that both Christopher John Spencer and his successor Richard Henry Wilkinson, appointed when the former moved to London (and played a pivotal role in the development of electric transport there subsequently), were both keen exponents of the trolleybus. Another similar figure was Charles Owen Silver, the general manager at Wolverhampton, who oversaw the development of the trolleybus network. Sometimes – as in the case of William Forbes at Cardiff and Stuart Pilcher at Manchester – the powers that be went over the opposition of the manager to see the introduction of trolleybuses. Later on, it was the vision, for example, of Chaceley Thornton Humpidge at Bradford and Ronald Edgley Cox at Walsall that saw some of the longer surviving systems prosper when others were being abandoned. However, for each Humpidge and Cox there were multiple figures like John C. Wake (who oversaw the conversions of both St Helens and Nottingham and was general manager at Bradford at the crucial time in 1961/62 when the future of the system was under active debate in the light of city centre redevelopment).

That the Bradford system was faced by redevelopment was an irony in terms of the trolleybus; when first introduced, the vehicles were perceived as a flexible alternative to the inflexible tram. Indeed, many early promotional photographs were designed to show this by recording vehicles undertaking dramatic overtaking movements. However, the trolleybus was still restricted, for the most part (the use of traction batteries by some operators gave some better flexibility) by its use of overhead; when one-way systems were developed or when city centres underwent wholesale redevelopment, replacement was costly. This led, in a certain number of cases, to the anachronistic – and generally short-term – operation of contraflow trolleybuses along new one-way streets. Moreover, the pressure for the construction of new housing estates in the suburbs – both to cater for slum clearance and for a growing population – meant that these were beyond the existing termini and were much more easily served by the motorbus.

One factor in the enthusiasm of many operators to adopt the trolleybus was the fact that many councils and companies also owned the power stations that generated the electricity used. There was a virtue in supporting your local power station – what today would be called vertical integration – and public transport provided a demand that made the generating of power more efficient. All this, however, was to change on 13 August 1947 when Royal Assent was given to the Electricity Act 1947. This Act saw the creation of the British Electricity Authority and, on 1 April 1948, more than 500 local authority and company owned electricity undertaking were vested into the newly Nationalised industry. There were exceptions; it was not until 1958, for example that Glasgow Corporation's Pinkston power station ceased to be municipally owned. There were two immediate consequences of the changed ownership and neither worked to the trolleybuses' advantage. Firstly, no longer could the general managers of the transport department and electricity department sit down and agree a price for the electricity used; in the future the trolleybus operators had to pay the market price. Secondly, the price of electricity rose inexorably, making the cheap diesel used by the motorbus all the more attractive.

By the 1960s, the number of suppliers of new trolleybuses had declined to only two, BUT and Sunbeam. Daimler supplied no further trolleybus chassis to British operators after the delivery of batches to Glasgow and Rotherham during 1950 and 1951. Guy Motors Ltd manufactured the last Guy-badged trolleybuses during 1949 and 1950 with a batch of 8ft 0in wide vehicles supplied – appropriately – to Wolverhampton Corporation; however, having acquired the Sunbeam Trolleybus Co Ltd in October 1948 (and closing its Moorfield Works five years later), Guy continued to produce Sunbeam-badged trolleybuses until 1966 although none were supplied to the British market after the delivery of Nos 295-303 to Bournemouth during 1962. These were the last first-generation trolleybuses supplied to any British operator. British United Traction Ltd (BUT) was a joint venture between AEC and Leyland established in 1946. Production was based, until 1948 (when due to declining demand the factory was closed), at Leyland's Kingston factory; thereafter double-deck production was based at Southall and single-deck at Leyland. Subsequently, some work was undertaken at the ex-Crossley works at Stockport. Production continued until 1964 but, by that date, the only orders were for the export market. One factor in the demise of the domestic market was the ready supply of second-hand vehicles as relatively new vehicles were disposed by some of the early post-war conversions; whilst this undoubtedly benefited operators such as Bradford and Walsall, who were able to strengthen their fleets at moderate cost, it did little to sustain the supply base.

It was not only the vehicle suppliers that disappeared; the surviving trolleybus operators needed a regular supply of replacement overhead and fittings. The decision of British Insulated Callender's Cables Ltd (BICC), one of the country's leading supplies of overhead equipment, to cease its production in the late 1960s was another factor in the final demise of the trolleybus. It became increasingly difficult to obtain spares and the condition of the overhead and trolleybuses with many fleets was poor towards their final closure. The lack of spares was often a reason cited for accelerating the final conversion, although when the author was involved in helping to recover the surviving spares from Thornbury depot following Bradford's final conversion in March 1972, there seemed to be a veritable Aladdin's Cave of fittings emerging.

Four systems survived into the 1970s; in the case of Cardiff, it more limped than survived as public services had ceased in December 1969 and only final tours operated in January 1970. Walsall had been subsumed into the West Midlands Passenger Transport Executive and whilst Edgley Cox had a senior role within the new body, it was unlikely that the trolleybus would survive long within a predominantly bus-based business. The transfer of ex-Birmingham buses saw the final elimination in two phases during 1970. The Teesside Railless Traction Board had also been integrated into a larger body – Teesside Municipal Transport – and, despite having opened the country's last extension on 31 March 1968 and having purchased five relatively new vehicles second-hand from Reading, was to be converted in April 1971.

This left Bradford – a case of the first also being the last. In June 1971, the sixtieth anniversary of the system was celebrated. This was a much more low-key event than that which marked the fiftieth anniversary in 1961. The mood was sombre as already moves were afoot for the final conversions. Although there had been no conversions since the Wakefield Road routes were replaced by motorbuses in 1967, the Allerton route – the city's first tram-to-trolleybus conversion (in 1929) and by that date the oldest surviving trolleybus route in the country – was converted to bus operation in February 1971. Over the next twelve months, the remainder of the system disappeared until – come March 1972 – only two routes remained operational. The final weekend – Friday 24 to Sunday 26 March – saw vast numbers of enthusiasts descend on the city to pay their final respects. Was that the end of the story? It might not have been had circumstances been different. The first oil crisis of the early 1970s highlighted the vulnerability of relying on imported oil – just as the Suez Crisis had done in 1956 – and the newly created West Yorkshire Metropolitan County Council did much to try and build a case for a new system. If plans had been carried through, the first routes to have seen trolleybuses restored as part of the council's policy would have been the services to Wibsey and Buttershaw. These plans came to nought as did plans a decade or so later to reintroduce trolleybuses to Leeds as a low-cost alternative to a rapid transit scheme.

AUTHOR'S NOTE

Within the specifications for each volume, each system history can only be a brief resume of the story; there are an increasing number of highly-detailed fleet histories and details of many of these can be found in the bibliography. Throughout the book, I have referred to 'trolleybuses'; in the early history they were often referred to as 'tracklesses' or 'trackless trams' whilst a further alternative was 'trolley vehicles'. For the sake of consistency, I have used the word 'trolleybus' throughout except when citing contemporary documentation when the original wording has been maintained. The maps are purely indicative of each network; one of the factors that made trolleybuses a popular alternative to the tram was the relative ease of erecting overhead and so many junctions and roads, particularly in town or city centres, varied over time. The maps thus show all roads that had – at some stage – trolleybus overhead; as a result, more complex systems will show sections that were not operated simultaneously. For example, with Bradford, the routes to Bolton Woods and Frizinghall, both closed in the early 1930s, are shown alongside routes such as those to Buttershaw, Holme Wood and Wibsey that opened between 1955 and 1960. There is a similar issue with route numbers; many operators did not use route letters or number originally and over a period of time the routes that did operate could change both in terms of termini and route number. The photographs used in this book have come from a variety of sources. Wherever possible, contributors have been identified, although some images may have been used without the correct attribution, and every effort made to try and identify current copyright holders in the event of the original photographer being deceased. In the event of any incorrect attribution, apologies are offered and full credit will be given in any future edition. Should this be the case, please make contact with author via the publishers.

ABERDARE

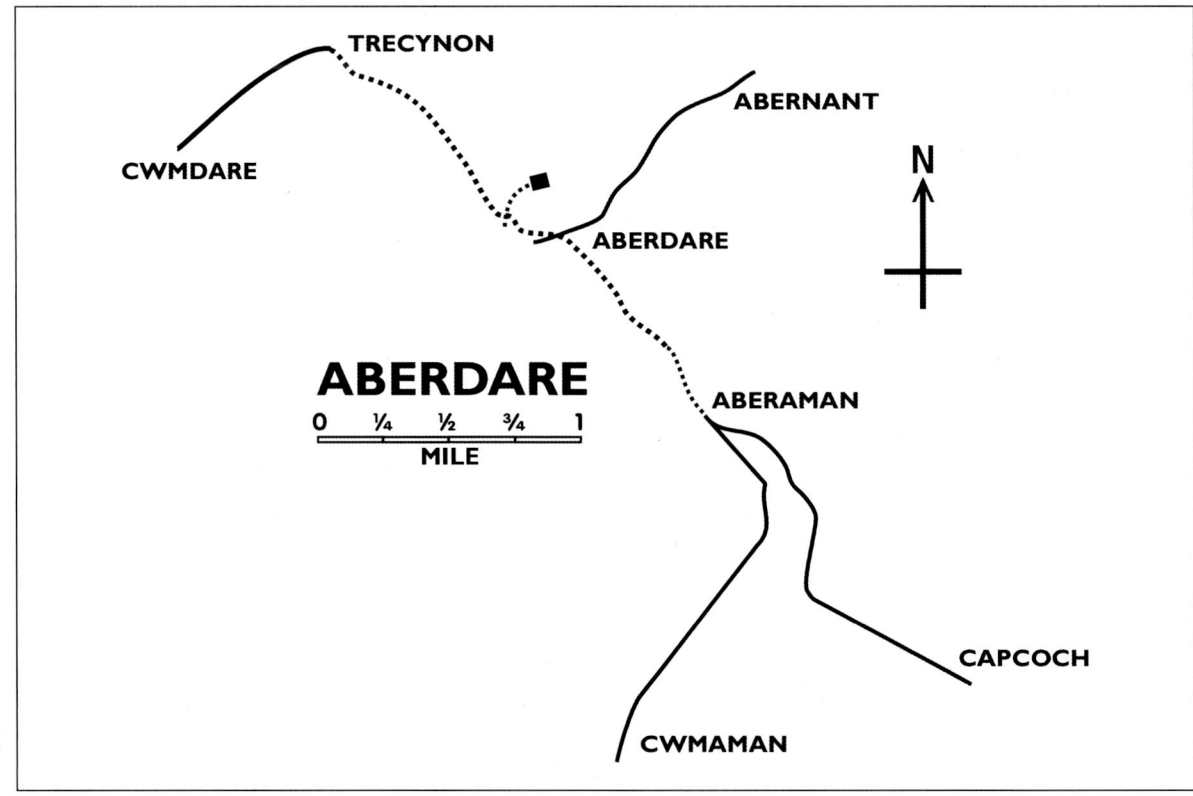

Although there had been proposals by BET in the late nineteenth century for the construction of an electric tramway to serve Aberdare, these had come to nothing and during the first decade of the twentieth century Aberdare UDC decided to apply for powers to construct its own tramway. In 1911 it obtained authorisation to build a single route – from Trycynon to Aberaman (a distance of 2¾ miles) – which was shorter than the original proposed route which would have extended further south to Abercwmboi.

Alongside the tramway plans, the UDC also decided to adopt trolleybuses to act as feeder routes to the main tramway and powers to operate trolleybuses was also included in the 1911 Act. Four routes were planned: from Trecynon to Cwmdare; Aberdare itself to Abernant; and from Aberaman to both Cymaman and Abercwmboi. The total trolleybus route mileage proposed was about 3½ miles.

Work on the construction of both the tramway and trolleybus routes proceeded concurrently. A trial run for the first trolleybus took place on 22 September 1913 and, following the inspection, the official opening occurred on 9 October 1913. Public tram operation commenced from that day, but it was not until 15 January 1914 that regular trolleybus services were introduced.

With St Elvan's church and one of the of ten single-deck four-wheel tramcars acquired for the system's opening (subsequently ten open-top double-deck trams were also acquired) in the background, the first of the eight Cedes-Stoll trolleybuses operated by Aberdare UDC stands at the junction of Commercial Street and Cannon Street in the town centre. Commercial Street was the terminus of the one-mile long route to Abernant. *F.K. Farrell Collection/Online Transport Archive*

As a pioneer in an era when the technology was still under development, Aberdare adopted the unusual Cedes-Stoll method of current collection; this system, developed in Austria, saw a small four-wheel trolley run on top of the overhead; this was linked by a detachable cable to the vehicle itself. This facility allowed for each route to be equipped, theoretically, with only a single line of overhead, with the trolleybuses exchanging trolleys when they passed each other. Of the four trolleybus routes, three were equipped with a single line of overhead with only the route to Cwmaman having a double set of wires.

Alongside the ten 3ft 6in gauge trams acquired for the new service, eight trolleybuses were also purchased; all vehicles were based at the UDC's new depot at Gadlys, in Aberdare, with the trolleybuses accessing the facility initially via a skate and the tram track and overhead. This arrangement was not to last long, with the trolleybuses eventually being towed to and from the depot.

One of the consequences of acquiring Austrian technology was that, during the First World War, it became impossible to obtain spare parts and the trolleybus services were only maintained in part through the ingenuity of the staff. However, by the end of the war only four trolleybuses remained operational and the routes to Cymaman and Abercwmboi had both effectively closed by 31 March 1919. The same year saw the UDC order its first motorbuses and these entered service on 12 November 1920.

Whilst the two routes from Aberaman were now operated by motorbus, the UDC decided to extend the tramway over the ex-trolleybus routes with a view to creating connections with the tramways in Pontypridd and Rhondda. Work started in April 1920 and the two routes – unique examples in Great Britain of a tramway being constructed in place of trolleybus routes – opened in 1922.

To operate the four short sections of route, Aberdare UDC acquired eight trolleybuses; all were equipped with twenty-seven-seat bodies supplied by Dodson. This view of No 25 shows to good effect the pole at the front offside used to connect the vehicle to the cable which, in turn, linked into the small four-wheel trolley that ran on the overhead. The supply of spare parts for the Austrian-built chassis inevitably proved difficult to obtain during the First World War with the result that the fleet declined, resulting in the effective abandonment of the two routes from Aberaman by March 1919. Only three trolleybuses remained operational in 1921 and this was reduced to two the following year. Although the council was offered replacement Cedes-Stoll trolleybuses by Keighley Corporation, this was declined. *Barry Cross Collection/Online Transport Archive*

The remaining trolleybuses soldiered on; however, the operational fleet had been reduced to three in 1921 and, in January 1923, the council effectively determined that the trolleybus routes be abandoned when it decided against the purchase of new vehicles and other significant expenditure.

During 1924 a further vehicle was withdrawn, and the final date of operation is uncertain; the demise of the system was recorded in the local newspaper on 8 August 1925 as 'The Cedes Stoll trolley vehicle has completely broken down'.

The report went on to comment that Keighley Corporation had offered replacement vehicles and that these were to be inspected. A month later, *Commercial Motor* was more confident about the future; it reported: 'Trackless trolley-buses are also to be acquired and an offer having been received from the Keighley (Yorks) council to sell to the Aberdare authority certain examples of this class of vehicle; a report has been called for from the manager [W.T. Hilder] as to the advisability of accepting the offer or treating direct with manufacturing firms.'

In the event nothing happened, and the pioneering Aberdare system was abandoned.

A side view of one of the trolleybuses when virtually brand new. The vehicle is seen posed in front of the depot at Gadlys, which was built to accommodate twelve trams and the eight trolleybuses. *John Meredith Collection/Online Transport Archive*

Fleet number	Registration	Chassis	Body	New	Withdrawn	Notes
21-28	N/A	Cedes Electric Traction Ltd	Dodson B27R	1913	1919-25	

Route number	From	To	Date Opened	Date Closed	Notes
N/A	Cwmdare	Trecynon	15 January 1914	July 1925	
N/A	Aberdare	Abernant	15 January 1914	July 1925	
N/A	Aberaman	Capcoch	15 January 1914	By 31 March 1919	
N/A	Aberaman	Cwmaman	15 January 1914	By 31 March 1919	

BIRMINGHAM

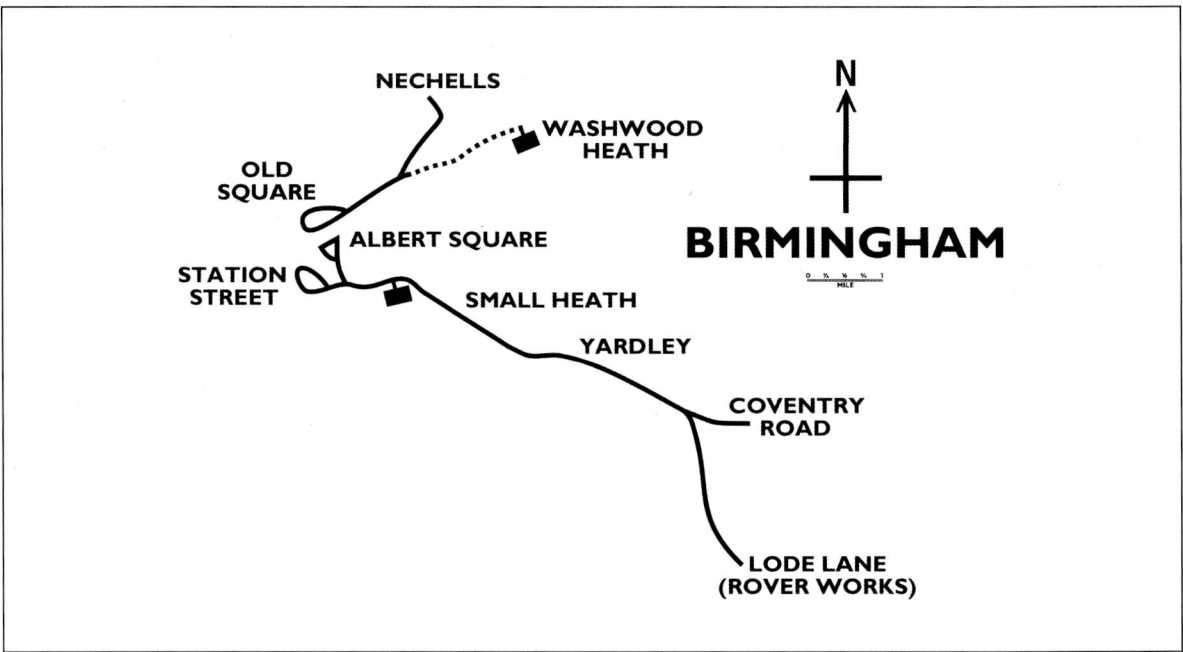

Although Birmingham Corporation promoted a Bill during the 1911-12 parliamentary session seeking powers to operate trolleybuses, the Bill was eventually withdrawn, and it was not until after the First World War that the possibility of introducing this type of transport would arise again.

By the early 1920s, the pioneering trolleybus systems had had a decade of experience of operation and the design of vehicles had evolved. In November 1920 Bradford Corporation had introduced the first top-covered trolleybus to service – No 521 – and early in 1922 this had been followed by a second – larger – three-axle vehicle, No 522, that could accommodate fifty-nine seated passengers; this capacity was similar to that which a contemporary tram could accommodate and so, for the first time perhaps, the trolleybus could be considered as a threat to existing tramways.

In 1921, representatives from Birmingham visited Bradford and saw the first double-decker in operation. Encouraged by what they saw, the members of Birmingham's tramway committee decided to introduce an experimental trolleybus service to replace the existing tram route to Nechells, which was considered to be life expired.

The success of the Bradford double-deckers had encouraged the Board of Trade to permit double-deck trolleybus operation with enclosed top decks. As a result, Birmingham placed an order for twelve chassis from Railless of Rochester which were to be fitted with fifty-one-seat double-deck bodies built by Charles H. Roe. Work

For the introduction of trolleybuses to the Nechells route – the first tram to trolleybus conversion in Britain – a batch of twelve Railless F12 fitted with Roe fifty-one-seat bodywork was acquired. The order had been placed in September 1921 and all were delivered prior to the introduction of services on the 2½-mile route from Old Square to Nechells. All were withdrawn during 1932 when the new Leyland TBD1s were delivered. *J. Joyce Collection/Online Transport Archive*

on conversion proceeded and powers to operate trolleybuses were enshrined in the Birmingham Corporation Act which received the Royal Assent on 4 August 1922.

On 27 November 1922, the new trolleybuses were introduced to the Old Square to Nechells service; the new route was about 2½ miles in length with the fleet being based at Washwood Heath depot, which was accessed by use of a skate allied to the existing tram track and overhead. Although the conversion of the Nechells route is generally regarded as the first complete tram-to-trolleybus conversion, the withdrawal of the Whitehall Road trams in Leeds – which had operated alongside the pioneering route from 1911 – earlier in the years makes the Leeds conversion technically the first.

The Nechells was, theoretically, an experiment but the rapid removal of the track meant that the restoration of the trams would have been well nigh impossible. For the next decade, the Nechells route operated in isolation; although its introduction had seen an improvement in the route's finances there was no further expansion until, in 1932, the future of tram services along Coventry Road came under consideration. By this stage, the original vehicles in use on the Nechells route had been replaced.

Like the Nechells route, the cost of upgrading the tramway along Coventry Road was not considered economic and, following the recommendation of the general manager, a decision was taken in May 1933 that trolleybuses be used in place of the trams. The service from the city centre – with its termini on Albert Square or Station Street – to

Yardley commenced operation with the vehicles supplied for its operation being allocated to Coventry Road depot, which they shared with the trams. The service was extended from Yardley to Sheldon on 5 July 1936.

Although the Birmingham tram system was to shrink considerably in the late 1930s, these subsequent conversions were all to motorbus and so, with the outbreak of war in September 1939, the system comprised only the routes to Nechells and to Sheldon. The former, however, was not to survive for long. The use of the skates with the tram track and overhead en route to and from the depot allied to arcing during operation are believed to have compromised the overnight blackout – and the Nechells area was a significant target locally for the Luftwaffe with its concentration of railways facilities and industry – with the result that it was decided to suspend operation of the route on 30 September 1940; the vehicles used were placed in store. During the war the overhead was cannibalised to permit running repairs elsewhere with the result that, come peace in 1945, the route was inoperable; it was thus decided to make its replacement by bus permanent and the stored vehicles were all disposed of for scrap.

Although the Nechells route disappeared during the war, there was to be one final extension to the system; this was the branch south to Lode Lane to serve the Rover works.

One of the more unusual of Birmingham's early trolleybuses was No 17; this was an AEC 607 fitted with a fifty-two-seat body supplied by Vickers. This was to be only double-deck trolleybus body built by Vickers – indeed their only other trolleybus bodies were a batch of twelve single-deckers supplied to Hartlepool – and, like the majority the Birmingham's early double-deckers, had rear open stairs. New in 1926, No 17 was withdrawn only six years later. *John Meredith Collection/Online Transport Archive*

The factory had been built in the late 1930s and the short extension to serve it opened on 29 October 1941.

After the war, the corporation reverted to its pre-war policy of tramcar conversion, again with the motorbus as the preferred means of replacement. The trolleybuses, however, soldiered on. In early 1949, a new loop was introduced to provide a short working to Lyndon Road, just short of the Sheldon terminus to relieve congestion. However, during the summer of 1949, it was decided that the city would cease the use of all electric traction – the fate of the trolleybuses was sealed.

The last full day of operation was 30 June 1951 with No 45 providing the last public service; No 90 was the official last trolleybus, reaching Coventry Road depot for the last time very early on 1 July 1951.

In 1932, Birmingham replaced its original fleet of trolleybuses. Amongst the vehicles acquired were eleven Leyland TBD1s fitted with Short-built bodywork. One of the batch – No 11 – is seen here in Old Square – the city terminus of the Nechells route. The Nechells route was suspended on 30 September 1940 when it was realised that arcing from the trolleyheads or from the use of skates when accessing the depot at Washwood Heath would cause problems during blackouts and, as the route served part of the city with obvious targets for the Luftwaffe (such the locomotive shed at Aston), the risk needed to be minimised. Following the suspension, the trolleybuses allocated to the Nechells service were stored; they were never to operate again. During the war, the overhead on the Nechells route was cannibalised in order to assist with necessary repairs caused by bomb damage to the tramway overhead and, when peace was restored in 1945, the condition of the overhead on the route was such as to preclude easy restoration and so it was abandoned. *Harry Luff Collection/Online Transport Archive*

Also acquired during 1932 were five AEC 663Ts – Nos 12-16 – fitted with Brush-built fifty-eight-seat bodywork. No 15 is pictured when new; all five were withdrawn in 1940 when the Nechells service was suspended and were never to operate again. *J. Joyce Collection/Online Transport Archive*

The trolleybuses used on the Coventry Road route were accommodated in the existing tram depot on Coventry Road in Bordesley. The depot, which dated originally to 1906, was also used to house trams until 2 October 1948. Heading outbound passed the depot is No 42; this was one of a batch of fifty trolleybuses – Nos 17-66 – that were new in 1933 prior to the conversion of the Coventry Road route on 7 January 1934. The new vehicles were all Leyland TTBD2s fitted with bodywork supplied by the locally-based MCCW; all remained in service until 1951. *W.S. Eades Collection/Online Transport Archive*

Above left: **In 1937,** Leyland supplied a batch of twelve trolleybuses – Nos 67-78; these were TB5s and were fitted with MCCW bodywork. On 3 June 1950, No 69 is seen heading inbound. All of the batch survived until July 1951. *John Meredith/Online Transport Archive*

Above right: **Looking in** superb external condition at Yardley on 3 June 1950, No 85 was one of twelve Leyland TB7s – Nos 79-90 – that were supplied in 1940. Fitted with MCCW bodywork, these were the last trolleybuses to be acquired by Birmingham and all were to survive until the final closure of the system in July 1951. *John Meredith/Online Transport Archive*

The last extension to the Birmingham system opened on 29 October 1941 when a branch from the Coventry Road route was opened southwards to serve the Rover factory at Lode Lane in Solihull. The factory, which had opened in 1939, was an important site for the manufacture of aircraft engines. Initially it had been served by Midland Red buses, but these used scarce fuel and an extension of the trolleybus system – despite the fact that it went beyond the Birmingham boundary – was deemed the most practical solution to getting workers to and from the factory. Initially the route operated only when the shift changed but subsequently a regular frequency service was introduced. On 17 June 1951, a fortnight before the system closed, the Southern Counties Touring Society organised a tour of the Birmingham system and here No 90 is seen at the Rover factory terminus. *John Meredith/Online Transport Archive*

With the tour vehicle, No 90, in the background on 17 June 1951, No 20 is pictured at the junction on Coventry Road with Lode Lane. No 90 is about to take the branch towards the Rover factory. No 20 was one of fifty Leyland TTBD2s – Nos 17-66 – that were supplied in 1934 for the conversion of the Coventry Road route. Fitted with MCCW bodywork all remained in service until 1951. *John Meredith/Online Transport Archive*

Two of the 1933 Leyland TTBD2s – with No 33 nearest to the camera – are recorded after withdrawal in 1951 as they make their last journey towards the scrapyard. *W.S. Eades Collection/Online Transport Archive*

BIRMINGHAM

Fleet number	Registration	Chassis	Body	New	Withdrawn	Notes
1-12	OK4823-4834	Railless F12	Roe H51RO	1922	1932	
13	OL994	AEC 602	Brush B36R	1923	1923	Demonstrator; returned to AEC August 1923
13	OL4636	EMB	Roe H48R	1924	1928	Demonstrator; returned to EMB June 1928
14-16	ON2825-2827	AEC 604	Short H51RO	1926	1932	
17	ON3261	AEC 607	Vickers H52RO	1926	1932	
18	UK8341	Guy BTX	Guy H53R	1930	1931	Demonstrator; returned to Guy May 1931; passed to Llanelly
19	OG9886	Guy BTX	Guy H53R	1931	1931	Guy demonstrator; passed to Llanelly
19	OV1175	Leyland TBD1	Short L48R	1931	1931	Leyland demonstrator
20	OV1194	Guy BT	Guy/PRV L48R	1931	1931	Leyland demonstrator
1-3, 5-7, 9-11, 13 and 15 (13 and 15 renumbered 4 and 8 in 1932)	OV4001-4003/ 4005-4007/ 4009-4011/ 4013/4015	Leyland TBD1	Short H48R	1932	1940	
12-16	OJ1012-1016	AEC 663T	Brush H58R	1932	1940	
17	TJ939	Leyland TTBD1	Leyland H60R	1933	1933	Leyland demonstrator
17-66	OC1117-1166	Leyland TTBD2	MCCW H58R	1934	1951	
68	TJ939	Leyland TTBD1	Leyland H60R	1933	1937	Ex-17 remotored; Leyland demonstrator
67-78	COX67-78	Leyland TB5	MCCW H53R	1937	1951	
79-90	FOK79-90	Leyland TB5	MCCW H54R	1940	1951	

Route number	From	To	Date Opened	Date Closed	Notes
7	City Centre (Old Square)	Nechells	27 November 1922	30 September 1940	Service suspended due to the Second World War and never reinstated.
92 and 93	City Centre (Albert Square or Station Street)	Yardley	7 January 1934	30 June 1951	93 became peak hours only in September 1939; section also served by route 56 and 57 that were peak hour services that operated to Hay Mills
94 and 95	Yardley	Sheldon	5 July 1936	30 June 1951	
96	Coventry Road	Lode Lane (Rover Works)	29 October 1941	30 June 1951	

Leyland TTBD2 No 32 is pictured at Yardley on 3 June 1950 prior to heading inbound with a service on route 94 towards Albert Square. *John Meredith/Online Transport Archive*

Pictured at the Yardley terminus of routes 94 and 95 is No 62. Note the Bundy clock on the pavement adjacent to the trolleybus; these devices were used by Birmingham Corporation, amongst others, at outlying termini in order to ensure timely departure by the crews. *H. Luff/Online Transport Archive*

On 10 July 1949 one of the 1934 batch of Leyland TTBD2s with MCCW bodywork – No 18 – is seen on Carr's Lane with a service on route 94. *C. Carter/Online Transport Archive*

CARDIFF

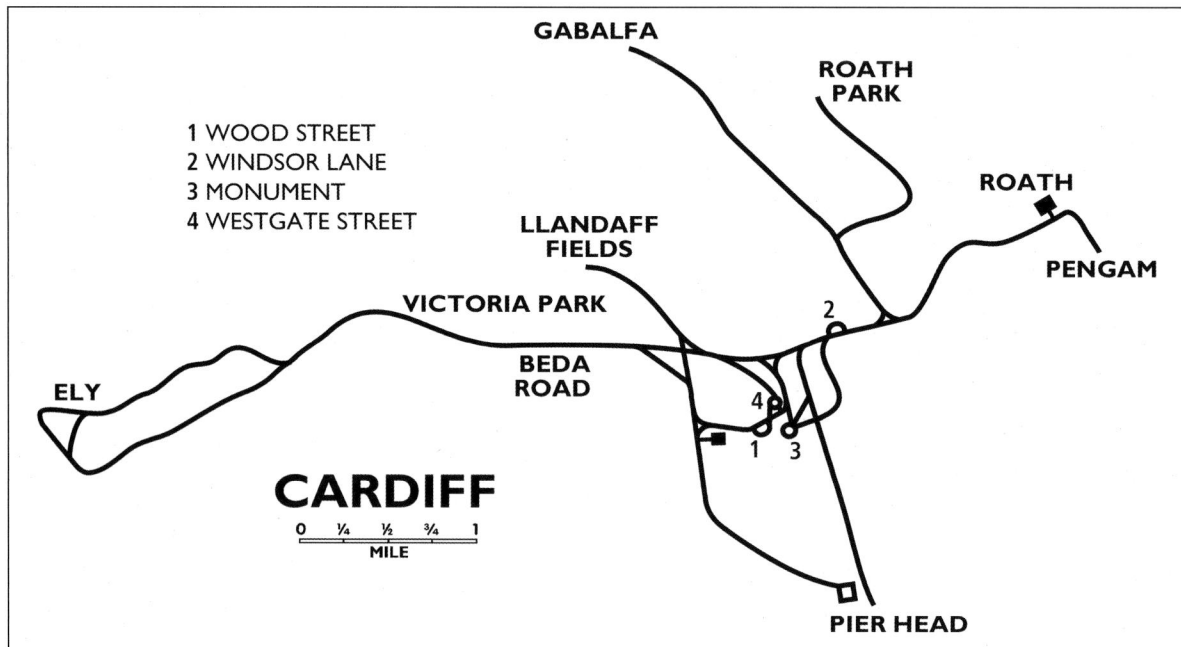

Following its acquisition of the existing company-owned horse tramways within the city, Cardiff Corporation introduced its first electric tramcars on 17 October 1902 and at its peak the network extended for 19½ route miles. As early as 1911, representatives of the corporation visited Bradford and Leeds and, in a report to the transport committee in October of that year, reported back favourably on their trip, commenting, 'We consider we should find profitable use for the Trackless Trolley System in Cardiff and its outskirts, in such districts as Whitchurch, Llanishen and Ely. It might also be found desirable in tapping districts within the City, which are not already served by our present Tramway.' Despite the positive report, there was to no progress at this stage, and it was to be more than quarter of a century before the possibility of the introduction of trolleybuses resurfaced.

One of the issues with the tramcar network was the number of low railway bridges; this had had the result of preventing the use of top-covered trams until the development of a lowbridge fully-enclosed double-deck tram in conjunction with Brush in the early 1920s. In 1920, Robert L. Horsfield was appointed general manager; under his aegis the bulk of the tramcar fleet was renewed and the last extension – to Gabalfa – was opened on 16 June 1928. However, in September 1928, Horsfield departed to become general manager at Leeds; he was succeeded by William Forbes from Aberdeen who was perceived to be pro-bus. However, given the relatively modern fleet there was little immediate pressure for the conversion of the tramway – other than the predominantly

For the opening of the Cardiff system on 1 March 1942, the corporation had received five AEC 661Ts fitted with Northern Counties lowheight sixty-seat bodywork. The first, incorrectly numbered 200 on delivery, was followed by Nos 202-05 to enable services to commence. The remainder of the batch of ten – Nos 206-10 – were delivered between October 1942 and February 1943; typical of the batch is No 206 seen here. The ten were withdrawn from service between September 1962 and June 1965 with No 203 being preserved on withdrawal in December 1962. *Harry Luff/Online Transport Archive*

single-track Cathays route that had been converted in 1929 – and it was not until towards the end of the next decade that the first inkling of tramway conversion was suggested and, initially, it was proposed that motorbuses be used to replace the trams through Wood Street although it was subsequently decided to relay the tram track.

During 1938 and 1939 there was a debate about tram replacement with reports on the various options being presented; Forbes was vehemently in favour of the motorbus whilst the city treasurer was pro-trolleybus. In the event, when it came to a vote on 8 May 1939, it was the pro-trolleybus group that won. Powers to replace the tram services by trolleybuses were already in place – they were enshrined in the Cardiff Corporation Act 1934 that had received the Royal Assent on 31 July 1934 – but these were extended by the Cardiff Corporation (Trolley Vehicles) Order Confirmation Act 1940, which received the Royal Assent on 17 July 1940. By this date the transport department was in the curious position of being jointly managed by the traffic manager, J.W. Dunning, and chief engineer, W.J. Evans; this persisted until 1946 when Evans departed to become general manager at Reading. Dunning died two years later and was succeeded by J.F. Siddall.

However, the outbreak of war in September 1939 meant that the conversion work on the initial service was delayed. Although Leyland had originally been contracted to supply ten trolleybuses, the company was not in a position to deliver them, having been instructed by the government to concentrate on military equipment, and it was not until 1941 that AEC as new supplier was able to deliver the first of the initial batch. Work on the overhead proceeded and, on 5 November 1941, the Wood Street to Pier Head section underwent its official Ministry of Transport inspection and, with additional vehicles now available, the new service was officially launched on 1 March 1942. The Cathedral Road service to Llandaff Fields was replaced by trolleybuses on 8 November 1942.

The trolleybuses were equipped for the pay-as-you-enter service with a flat fare of 1d; the success of the system saw it extended to the tram services and to certain motorbus services as well. However, post-war inflation meant that the system was unsustainable and it was replaced by the more common Ultimate ticketing system on 12 November 1950. Another facet of all of the double-deckers operated by Cardiff was their low – 15ft 0in – height to cater for some of the low bridges.

There were to be no further tram-to-trolleybus conversions during the war and the next route to be converted – that to Pier Head via Bute Street – was initially converted to motorbus operation on 27 April 1946. On 1 August 1946, the Cardiff Corporation Act 1946 received the Royal Assent; this granted additional powers to operate trolleybuses.

Pictured in Bute Town is No 236; this was one of seven single-deckers – Nos 231-37 – that were acquired from Pontypridd UDC in 1947. These vehicles had been rendered surplus with the UDC as a result of the delivery of a number of Karrier Ws during 1945 and 1946 and had been offered for sale. Recognising that, in the post-war era of austerity that it might be useful to obtain additional vehicles as deliveries of new vehicles might be restricted, Cardiff acquired the seven vehicles with their operation largely restricted to the Pier Head via Bute Street service as a result of a low railway bridge. Their time in Cardiff was, however, to be relatively limited as all seven were withdrawn between May 1949 and August 1950. *F.N.T. Lloyd-Jones/Online Transport Archive*

The Pier Head route, due to the low railway bridge in Bute Street, could only be operated by single-deckers and so, when trolleybus services were introduced on 17 August 1947, a batch of seven 1930-vintage single-deckers acquired from Pontypridd UDC took over operation; these were replaced two years later by five – later six – BUT 9641T single-deckers fitted with East Lancs bodywork.

The next tramway service to be converted was that to Victoria Park (Canton), where trolleybuses took over the service on 6 June 1948. The services along Newport Road were last operated by tram on 16 October 1948 with motorbuses taking over initially. The tram service to Roath Park was replaced by trolleybuses on 4 December 1949 with that along Whitchurch Road to Gabalfa following on 20 February 1950; the last trams in passenger service had operated the previous day and, on the 20th, tram No 11 operated all day suitably decorated to mark the final closure of the tramway system. The final ex-tram route to be converted to trolleybus operation was that along Newport Road to Royal Oak where trolleybuses were introduced on 15 October 1950; the service was extended beyond the original terminus to serve Pengam at the same time.

The first half of the 1950s saw few developments although, on 25 October 1953, the depot on Clare Road was closed on grounds of economy; all trolleybuses were thereafter

Cardiff No 211, seen here on Queen Street on 11 June 1952, was the first a batch of twenty BUT 9641Ts fitted with East Lancs sixty-seven-seat bodywork that were new originally in 1948; like all of the post-war deliveries, these vehicles were built to the new standard 8ft 0in width. The bodywork was the result of co-operation between the chief engineer, W.J. Evans, and the bodybuilder to create a vehicle suitable for Cardiff's specific needs: a pay as you enter system and the preponderance of low railway bridges. The resulting vehicles were 15ft 0in in height and included rear entrance with front exit and twin staircases. Eventually all were modified with the front exit doors panelled over. Withdrawal of the batch commenced in September 1962 but four of the batch – No 215/18/20/27 – survived until the end of the system. *C. Carter/Online Transport Archive*

A second batch of BUT 9641Ts – Nos 221-30 – was delivered during 1949 and here the last of the series is pictured outside the corporation's main depot on Newport Road. This view shows to good effect the rear entrance and front exit with which the East Lancs bodies were originally equipped. As with the first batch all – except No 222 – were modified with the front exit doors panelled over. This batch was withdrawn between April 1966 and December 1969. *Harry Luff/Online Transport Archive*

based at Roath depot at the end of the Newport Road route. There was, however, to be one final extension to the trolleybus network – the already authorised route westwards from Victoria Park to Ely – for which approval was given by the council in February 1953; following construction work, the new route was opened on 8 May 1955. The same year saw the delivery of a final batch of BUT 9641Ts; Nos 275-87 were destined to be the last new trolleybuses acquired by Cardiff. This took the trolleybus fleet to its maximum size: seventy-three double-deckers and six single-deckers.

By the late 1950s and early 1960s Cardiff, like other operators, was reviewing the future of its trolleybus system. In 1961 Siddall produced a balanced report in which he concluded that a phased replacement over ten years would allow for the optimum life of the fleet. This recommendation was agreed by the full council on 6 November 1961. As elsewhere, the trolleybuses were partially a victim of the desire to redevelop the city centre and various road improvement schemes.

The first route to be converted – on 24 November 1962 – was the extension of the Newport Road route beyond Royal Oak to Pengam. This was followed on by the conversion of the service to Pier Head via Bute Street on 11 January 1964; this resulted in the withdrawal of the six single-deckers. The second route to Pier Head – via Clarence

Road – was the next to succumb, on 16 December 1965 when a new weight limit was imposed on the Wood Street bridge. During 1965 a new one-way system in the city centre resulted in eastbound trolleybuses being diverted from Queen Street to operate via Kingsway, Cathays Park Road and Dumfries Place. The Llandaff Fields services were converted on 16 April 1966 (route 6) and 17 September 1966 (route 4) and, by the end of that year, the trolleybus fleet had shrunk to only forty-one vehicles.

There were to be no conversions during 1967 but two routes were converted during the following year. The Newport Road route was converted on 17 February, although the overhead was retained for depot workings to and from Roath, whilst on 27 April the Roath Park and Gabalfa routes followed. This left only one service surviving – that to Ely via Victoria Park – which, despite service problems caused by the deteriorating condition of both vehicles and overhead, was to survive until 3 December 1969, when the last timetabled passenger services operated. This was not, however, quite the end of the system as original plans had envisaged a last trolleybus week during January 1970. As a result, a special trolleybus service was operated on 9 and 10 January 1970 with No 262 acting as the official last trolleybus on the 11th with No 277 following it in. Of the Cardiff fleet, four examples – the last single-decker, No 243, and three double-deckers – survive in preservation.

In order to replace the ex-Pontypridd trolleybuses on route 16 to the Pier Head via Bute Street, five BUT 9641Ts – Nos 238-42 – equipped with East Lancs thirty-eight-seat single-deck bodies entered service during July and August 1949. With the Mill Lane premises of the stained glass manufacturer Bristow Wadley behind it, No 240 is pictured awaiting departure with a service. All of the batch were withdrawn as a result of the conversion of the route via Bute Road on 11 January 1964. *Marcus Eavis/Online Transport Archive*

Recorded in September 1964 awaiting departure with a service on route 5B towards Victoria Park is No 248; this was one of a further twenty BUT 9641Ts – Nos 245-64 – that were fitted with East Lancs-built bodywork. New between November 1949 and March 1950, these vehicles were also equipped with rear entrances and front exits when new but subsequently had the front exits panelled over. All of the batch were taken out of service between April 1965 and February 1969 with No 262 surviving into preservation. *Marcus Eavis/Online Transport Archive*

The final batch of trolleybuses delivered to Cardiff with the rear entrance/front exit bodywork was represented by ten more BUT 9641Ts – Nos 265-74 – that entered service between August and October 1950; the arrival of this and the previous batch coincided with the opening of the routes that served Pengam via Royal Oak. Again, all were eventually to have their front exits panelled over and were to be withdrawn between July 1965 and February 1969. *Harry Luff/Online Transport Archive*

Cardiff's last new double-deckers were thirteen BUT 9641Ts – Nos 275-87 – that were delivered between January and March 1955 to supplement the fleet for the extension from Victoria Park to Ely, which opened on 8 May 1955. Although again bodied by East Lancs, the loss of the front exit meant that the seating capacity was increased to seventy-two. With the exception of No 280, which was withdrawn following an accident in October 1968, all of the batch survived to be withdrawn between June 1969 and January 1970. *Marcus Eavis/Online Transport Archive*

In order to supplement the number of single-deckers available for the Bute Street route, one further BUT 9641T – No 243 – was purchased in 1955. Fitted with East Lancs bodywork, the decision not to incorporate a front exit meant that the seating capacity was increased to forty. This was to be the last three-axle trolleybus constructed for use in Britain as well as being the last trolleybus delivered to Cardiff; technically, due to relaxed regulations, it could have been constructed with only two axles for the same length but, for reasons of standardisation, the three-axle chassis was selected. Like Nos 238-42, No 243 was withdrawn following the conversion of the Bute Street route; however, unlike the other single-deckers, it was secured for preservation on withdrawal. *Marcus Eavis/Online Transport Archive*

Fleet number	Registration	Chassis	Body	New	Withdrawn	Notes
201-10	CKG191-200	AEC 6641T	Northern Counties L60R	1941-43	1962-65	201 erroneously numbered 200 when delivered but soon corrected; 203 preserved
211-30	DBO471-480/ DUH216-225	BUT 9641T	East Lancs L57D	1948	1966-70	215 preserved
231-37	TG379/381/383/ 385/387/389/391	EE	EE B32C	1930	1949-50	Ex-Pontypridd 1-7; acquired 1947
238-42	EBO891-895	BUT 9641T	East Lancs B38D	1949	1964	
243	KBO961	BUT 9641T	East Lancs B40R	1955	1964	Preserved
245-64	EBO902-921	BUT 9641T	East Lancs L67D	1949-50	1965-69	262 preserved
265-74	FBO85-94	BUT 9641T	East Lancs L67D	1950	1965-68	
275-87	KBO948-960	BUT 9641T	East Lancs L72R	1955	1968-70	

Route number	From	To	Date Opened	Date Closed	Notes
6/9	City Centre (Wood Street)	Pier Head (Clarence Road)	1 March 1942	16 December 1965	When Clarence Road section converted routes 6 and 9 cut back to Wood Street
16 (Renumbered 14 1 July 1962)	City Centre	Pier Head (via Bute Street)	17 August 1947	11 January 1964	
4/6	City Centre	Llandaff Fields	8 November 1942	17 September 1966	Route 6 converted on 16 April 1966
2A/5/5A/5B	City Centre	Victoria Park	6 June 1948	3 December 1969	2A operated from Pengam (ceased operation 24 November 1962); 5 ran from Windsor Lane (commenced 4 July 1948); 5A operated via Neville Street; 5B via Castle Street; 5/5A/5B ceased operation 22 July 1965
3/4	City Centre	Roath Park	4 December 1949	27 April 1968	Route 4 replaced 16 April 1966 with conversion of Llandaff Fields section

Route number	From	To	Date Opened	Date Closed	Notes
1/9	City Centre	Gabalfa (Whitchurch Road)	20 February 1950	27 April 1968	
2/2A/8	City Centre	Royal Oak (Newport Road)	15 October 1950	17 February 1968	
2/2A	Royal Oak (Newport Road)	Pengam	15 October 1950	24 November 1962	
10A/10B	Victoria Park	Ely (Greenfarm Road)	8 May 1955	3 December 1969	Date of last public services; final 'Last Trolleybus Week' services operated 9-10 January 1970

Pictured on 3 September 1968 is No 281 with a service on route 10A to Havelock Street. The trolleybus is pictured on Greenfarm Road, Ely; the section west from Victoria Park to Greenfarm Road was the last route extension to be opened in Cardiff – on 8 May 1955 – and was to become the city's last route. Although normal services ceased on 3 December 1969 (earlier than planned due to an industrial dispute with workshop staff at Roath), three days of special services were operated between 9 and 11 January 1970 between Victoria Park and Havelock Street as 11 January was the date originally planned for the system's final abandonment. When normal services ceased in December, there were only ten operational trolleybuses; these included No 281, which was one of a handful to remain available in January 1970. *Geoffrey Tribe/Online Transport Archive*

CHESTERFIELD

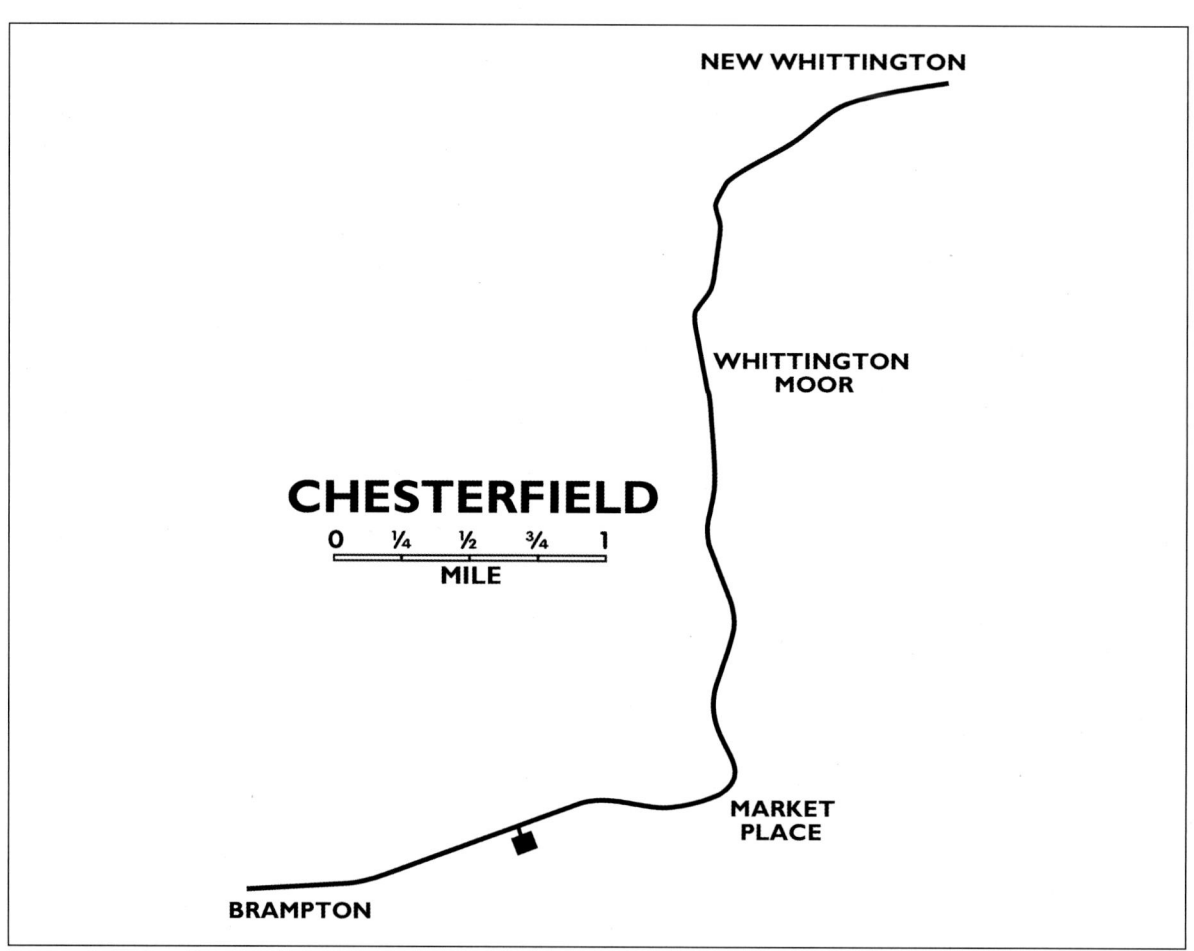

Chesterfield possessed a single standard gauge tramway; this linked Brampton via the town centre with Whittington. However, there were other parts of the town without public transport and, in 1912, the council decided to obtain powers to operate trolleybuses. On 15 August 1913 Royal Assent was given to the Chesterfield Corporation Railless Traction Act. This permitted the corporation to introduce trolleybuses to five routes – radiating out to Clay Cross to the south, Temple Normanton to the south-east, Brimington to the north-east, Unstone to the north and Newbold to the north-west – that would act as feeders to the existing tram route.

However, little was done to progress matters and, in February 1914 in a further move of apparent procrastination, it was decided to introduce motorbuses to the planned trolleybus routes in order to gauge potential demand. The First World War added to the delays and, in August 1922, it was decided to amend the powers to enable trolleybuses to

replace the trams; these were enshrined in the Chesterfield Corporation Act that received the Royal Assent on 2 August 1923.

Again little progressed immediately, although a visit was made to Birmingham to see the recently converted Nechells route. However, by the mid-1920s, the question of the future of the one tram route was beginning to become important and it was decided to replace it with trolleybuses. An order was placed with Straker-Clough for fourteen single-deckers; the bodywork was ordered from the locally-based Reeve & Kenning – the only trolleybus bodies that the company built. In order to accommodate the trolleybuses a new depot was constructed at Thornfield, Stonegavels, which replaced the original corporation tram depot at Chatsworth Road, which closed following the demise of the trams.

Work on modifying the overhead commenced in February 1927 with the first of the new trolleybuses being delivered two months later. Following driver training at Rotherham, the first services were introduced to the town centre to Brampton on 23 May 1927 following the official Board of Trade inspection four days earlier. The section from the town centre to Whittington Moor opened on 27 September 1927; this took the total length of the route to 3¾ miles.

In October 1927, it was agreed to undertake a two-mile extension from Whittington Moor to New Whittington; this opened on 29 July 1929. The fleet was increased by the purchase of two double-deckers in 1931. Two years later more than half the overhead was renewed with the then general manager – R. Hoggard – expressing confidence in

Chesterfield Corporation's first trolleybuses were a batch of fourteen – Nos 1-12/14/15 – supplied by Straker-Clough with Reeve & Kenning thirty-two-seat single-deck bodies. Pictured in 1927, when newly in service, No 12 stands at the terminus in Brampton. The section from the town centre to Brampton was the first to open – on 23 May 1927. *Barry Cross Collection/ Online Transport Archive*

A second of the initial batch – No 10 – is recorded here at the original terminus at Whittington Moor shortly the introduction of trolleybuses to the section on 27 September 1927. The only extension to the Chesterfield system saw the Whittington Moor route extended to New Whittington on 29 July 1929. *Barry Cross Collection/ Online Transport Archive*

Chesterfield Corporation operated three double-deck trolleybuses; two of these – Nos 16 and 17 (the former illustrated here) – were supplied by Ransomes in 1931. The third was a Leyland demonstrator used for four months the same year. The two Ransomes-built vehicles were both withdrawn in 1938. *W.J. Haynes*

the trolleybus, describing the network as 'efficient, reliable, safe and [able] to inspire confidence in a densely populated area.'

Taking advantage of the demise of the York system in 1935, Chesterfield acquired three three-year-old single-deckers; these were to be the last trolleybuses acquired as, in 1937, the corporation decided to convert the one route to bus operation. The reasons for this were given by Mr Hoggard in an interview in February 1938. Amongst the factors cited were problems with the GPO's telephone cabling, the age of much of the overhead equipment (despite the 1933 rewiring much dated back to the introduction of the trams during 1904 and 1905), the number of low railway bridges (which precluded extending the trolleybus network to other routes) and the cost of electricity.

The final Chesterfield trolleybuses operated on 24 March 1938; the redundant fleet was then stored in a field by the depot until the summer when they were sold for scrap. The sale of the vehicles raised the sum of £80 (about £5,420 at current values) – not a bad return when it is considered that all investment in the trolleybus system had been written off by the time it was decided to convert the system (another factor, according to Mr Hoggard, in the decision to abandon the system).

A forlorn picture taken in 1938, after the cessation of trolleybus operation on 24 March of that year, sees the Chesterfield fleet awaiting final disposal. Closest to the camera are two of the original batch of trolleybuses supplied in 1927; alongside are the two double-deckers that were supplied by Ransomes in 1931 – Nos 16 and 17 (the latter on the right) – with the same manufacturer's forty-eight-seat bodywork. *J. Joyce Collection/Online Transport Archive*

Fleet number	Registration	Chassis	Body	New	Withdrawn	Notes
1-12/14/15	RA1810-1817/ 1819-1824	Straker-Clough	Reeve & Kenning B32C	1927	1938	
16 and 17	RB4890-4891	Ransomes D2	Ransomes L48R	1931	1938	
19	OV1175	Leyland TBD1	Short L48R	1931	1931	Leyland demonstrator used on hire for four months
18-20	VY2991-2993	Karrier-Clough E4S	Roe B32R	1932	1938	Ex-York 30-32; acquired 1935

Route number	From	To	Date Opened	Date Closed	Notes
N/A	Town Centre (Market Place)	Brampton	23 May 1927	24 March 1938	
N/A	Town Centre (Market Place)	Whittington Moor	27 September 1927	24 March 1938	
N/A	Whittington Moor	New Whittington	29 July 1929	24 March 1938	

DERBY

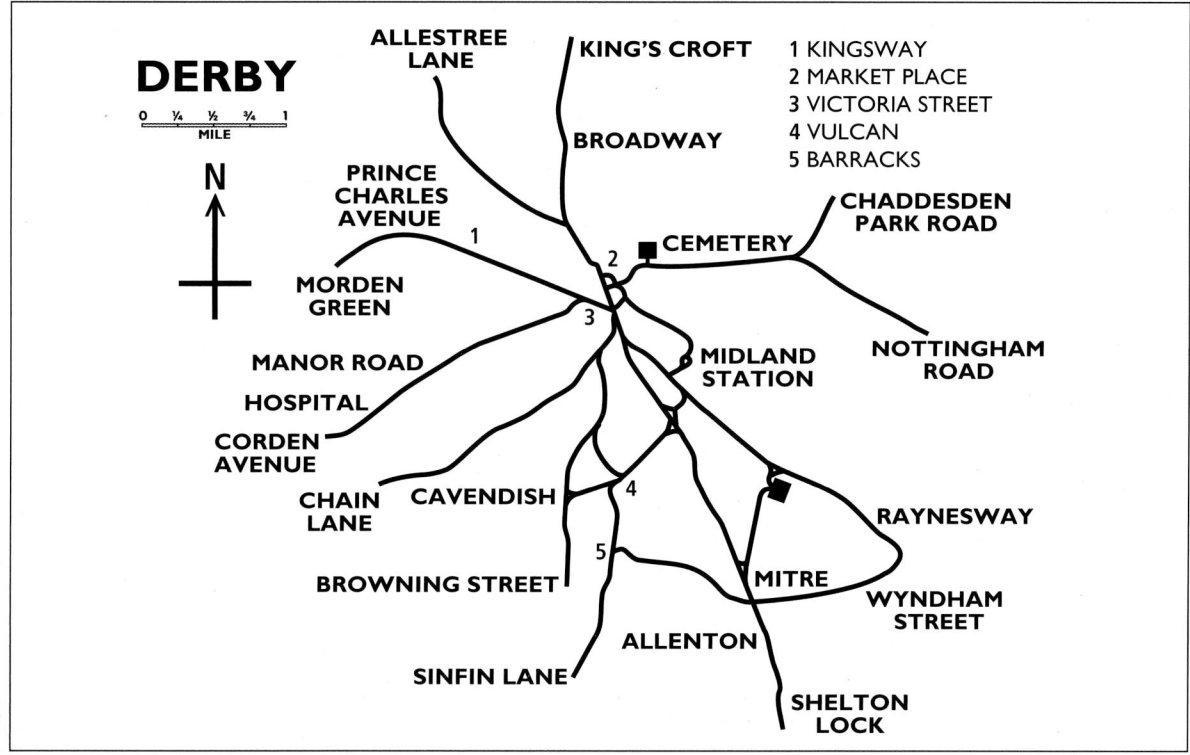

Having acquired the city's horse tramway network, Derby Corporation undertook the conversion of the 4ft 0in gauge system and its electrification. The first electric trams operated on 27 July 1904 and eventually served a network of almost fourteen route miles. As early as 1913, with the Derby Corporation Act 1913 that received the Royal Assent on 15 August 1913, powers were obtained for the operation of trolleybuses alongside additional tramway powers. However, nothing further was done at this stage to introduce trolleybuses.

By the late 1920s, the tramway system was increasingly dated, even though twenty-eight new trams had been delivered between 1920 and 1928, and consideration as to its future resulted in a committee being established to advise in 1929. The following year the recommendation was that the trams be replaced by trolleybuses and powers to undertake this were enshrined in the Derby Corporation Act 1930, which received the Royal Assent on 4 June 1930.

The first route to be converted was that along Nottingham Road which was at the same time to be extended beyond the original tram terminus at Wiltshire Road to the Creamery. In order to facilitate the conversion, the tram service was temporarily converted to motorbus operation from 16 November 1930. Following the erection of the overhead,

Pictured at Market Place in 1951 towards the end of its life – it was withdrawn later that year – is No 129; this was one of a batch of twenty Guy BTXs delivered during 1933. The arrival of Nos 115-34 facilitated the conversion of the Burton Road and Uttoxeter Road tram services during August 1933.
C. Carter/Online Transport Archive

the first test run occurred on 24 November 1931 with the official Ministry of Transport inspection being carried out on 4 January 1932. With the installation approved, the 2½-mile route was officially opened on 9 January 1932. The initial batch of six vehicles – Nos 79-84 (the highest numbered tram was No 78) – were based in the corporation's existing Nottingham Road tram depot.

Further deliveries of trolleybuses during 1932 permitted the conversion of the routes along London Road to Alvaston (extended to Wyndham Street) and along Osmaston Road on 24 July 1932 and 13 November 1932 respectively. The latter route had provided a cross-city service to Nottingham Road prior to the conversion in 1931 and from November 1932 this link was restored. In 1932 the tram services along Burton Road and Uttoxeter Road were converted to motorbus operation temporarily; the two were converted to trolleybus operation on 13 August 1933, being extended beyond the original tram termini at the same time. This was followed on 31 December 1933 by the conversion of the Ashbourne Road route. A further fifty-seven new trolleybuses were delivered between 1933 and 1936.

The last tram route was that serving Normanton Road; although tram services largely ceased in March 1934, occasional trams continued to operate until June and the official last tramcar operated on 2 July 1934. Trolleybuses had largely operated the Victoria Street via Cavendish to Midland Station route from 18 March 1934.

The period between 1934 and the outbreak of the Second World War was to see the continuing expansion of the system. The last of the ex-tram routes – that along Kedleston

Road that had been temporarily converted to motorbus – became trolleybus operated on 28 April 1935. The line from Cavendish Hotel to Browning Circle opened on 30 June 1935. Additional powers were granted courtesy of the Derby Corporation (Trolley Vehicles) Provisional Order Act 1936, which received the Royal Assent on 5 May 1936. On 29 November 1936, the branch off the Nottingham Road route to Chaddesden Park Road opened as did the section along Osmaston Park Road. Two final extensions – along Duffield Road to Broadway and from Allenton (Osmaston Road) to Shelton Lock – were opened on 11 July 1937 and 6 November 1938 respectively.

By the outbreak of war in September 1939. the fleet had grown to eighty-six double-deckers, the majority being Guy BTXs although the six most recent acquisitions – Nos 159-64 – were Daimler CTM4s, the only Daimler trolleybuses in the fleet. In order to cater for additional traffic during the war, the corporation acquired six additional Guy BTXs from Hastings & District; these were to prove the only single-deckers operated by Derby. There was to be one wartime extension with the opening of the section to Sinfin, with its various industrial employers, on 30 August 1943. This supplemented the motorbus service and thus reduced the use of diesel.

After the war, further powers were obtained in the Derby Corporation (Trolley Vehicles) Provisional Order Act 1946, which received the Royal Assent on 15 May 1946. This along with the delivery of fifteen semi-Utility bodied Sunbeam Ws between 1944, and 1946 permitted the extension of the Duffield Road route from Broadway to King's Croft on 14 September 1947. The same year saw the retirement of Percy Bancroft, the general manager who had overseen the introduction of the trolleybuses, and his replacement by John Firth, who had been appointed deputy general manager in 1942.

Between 1933 and 1936 the corporation acquired a total of fifty-six Guy BTXs – Nos 102-13/15-58 – fitted with Brush fifty-six-seat bodywork. No 137, which is pictured prior to operating a service on route 35 to Cavendish via Dairyhouse Road, was one of ten delivered during 1934 that permitted the withdrawal of the final trams. All were withdrawn between 1948 and 1953; No 137 was one of those taken out of service in 1951. *C.F. Klapper/The Bus Archive*

The first contraction occurred on 11 June 1950 when trolleybuses ceased to serve Chaddesden Park Road, with the service being integrated into the Wood Road bus service. However, the overhead was left intact and remained useable by workmen's specials until the final conversion of the Nottingham Road route in 1962. Further powers in the Derby Corporation (Trolley Vehicles) Provisional Order Act 1952, which received the Royal Assent on 15 May 1952, saw two final extensions opened; these were of the Ashbourne Road route in two stages to Prince Charles Avenue on 8 June 1952 and thence to Morden Green on 26 July 1953. There was to be one final extension – along Ascot Drive in April 1958 – to serve the new depot, but this never carried a passenger service. This took the network to almost twenty-eight route miles.

The new manager faced a number of issues. One was the increasing age of the fleet. This was partially alleviated by the delivery of fifty new trolleybuses between 1948 and 1953. The second problem – as elsewhere – was the need to expand services beyond the existing termini. As early as his annual report in 1953 saw Firth note that the operation of motorbus services to the new suburban estates would inevitably lead to the abstraction of traffic on those existing but parallel trolleybus routes. There were plans for the expansion of the trolleybus network but opposition to these, expressed volubly in a public inquiry in mid-1955, effectively sounded the death-knell for a mode of transport that was deemed increasingly outdated.

The final batch of Guy BTXs – Nos 149-58 – were new in 1936 and 1937. Two new trolleybus routes – to Chaddesden Park Road and Osmaston park Road – opened that year. The ten were withdrawn between 1949 and 1953; No 149, the first of the batch, is seen here awaiting disposal following withdrawal in 1951. *Harry Luff/Online Transport Archive*

During 1959 and 1960 the corporation took delivery of its final new trolleybuses – eight Sunbeam F4As fitted with Roe bodywork – but on 30 January 1960 the Browning Circle route beyond Cavendish Hotel was converted to motorbus operation to be followed on 10 November 1962 by the pioneering trolleybus route along Nottingham Road. The system's fate was sealed on 27 July 1963 when it was decided, largely as a result of major road works and city centre redevelopment along with the fact that the overhead infrastructure was going to need major investment, that the entire system be replaced by motorbus. The actual closure process was, however, complicated by the fact inadequate bus drivers meant that occasional trolleybus services were operated on notionally converted routes for a period after the official date of conversion.

The programme to eliminate the trolleybuses commenced on 3 October 1964 with the conversion of the King's Croft to Burton Road service. This was followed on 1 January 1966 by the withdrawal of trolleybuses to Sinfin – although the section was used occasionally until 3 April 1966 – and to Wyndham Street – although again the overhead remained for other services. On 26 November 1966, the service along Uttoxeter Road along with the Cavendish Hotel circular and the link from Victoria Street to the Midland station were converted. The penultimate conversion – on 11 February 1967 – saw motorbuses take over operation of the Kedleston Road route.

Trolleybus operation in Derby came to an end on 9 September 1967 with the conversion of the remaining services. The last trolleybus in public service – Nos 236 – arrived back at Ascot Drive depot just after midnight on the morning of the 10th. Of the Derby fleet, five examples, including two of the Utility-bodied Sunbeam Ws, survive in preservation.

Pictured inside Ascot Drive depot on 26 July 1953 is No 162. This was one of a batch of six Daimler CTM4s that were delivered in 1938 – the last new trolleybuses acquired by Derby prior to the Second World War – that were fitted with Brush fifty-four-seat bodies. With the exception of No 161, which was withdrawn in 1959, all were taken out of service during 1960. Ascot Drive depot was originally opened for the corporation's motorbus fleet in 1949 and was only adapted for trolleybus use subsequently. *John Meredith/Online Transport Archive*

Above: **In 1942**, in order to cater for the additional traffic that the war had generated, Derby acquired six second-hand Ransomes from Hastings & District. Nos 165-70 were to be the only single-deck trolleybuses operated in Derby and were destined for a short life – indeed only four actually entered service. This view of No 169 records the vehicle towards the end of its life at the Ormiston Road depot; it still bears the wartime white-painted mudguards that were designed to be an aid to visibility during the blackout. *W. J. Haynes*

Right: **Between 1944** and 1946, Derby was allocated fifteen Sunbeam Ws; these were fitted with either Weymann or Park Royal Utility fifty-six-seat bodywork. The first two – Nos 171 and 172 – were bodied by Weymann and retained their original bodywork through to withdrawal in 1964. Here No 171 is pictured inside the new Ascot Drive depot alongside one of the Sunbeam F4s delivered in 1952. Following withdrawal, No 172 was preserved. *Harry Luff/Online Transport Archive*

Left: **No 175** – pictured at the Shelton Lock terminus of route 66 prior heading to Nottingham Road – was one of three Sunbeam Ws delivered during 1945 that were fitted with semi-Utility bodywork supplied by Park Royal. No 173 was withdrawn during 1963 with the remaining two following the next year; No 175 was preserved following withdrawal. The cross-city service to Nottingham Road was introduced on 13 November 1932 and survived until the end of the Nottingham Road section on 10 November 1962; thereafter the Allenton route was renumbered 60 and terminated at the Market Square. *J. Joyce/Online Transport Archive*

Below: **On 12 May** 1964, No 178 awaits departure from the ex-Midland Railway station. This was one of fifteen Sunbeam Ws supplied between 1944 and 1946 that were fitted with Utility or semi-Utility fifty-six-seat bodywork by Weymann and Park Royal; never rebodied, by the date of their withdrawal – all were taken out of service between 1963 and 1966 – these were the last Utility-bodied trolleybuses still in service in the country. *C. Carter/Online Transport Archive*

48 • BRITISH TROLLEYBUS SYSTEMS – WALES, MIDLANDS AND EAST ANGLIA

Above: **During 1948** and 1949, Derby took delivery of a batch of thirty Brush-bodied Sunbeam F4s; the arrival of Nos 186-215 permitted the withdrawal of the twenty Guy BTXs that were new in 1932 whilst also facilitating the expansion of the fleet following the extension of the Duffield Road route to King's Croft (opened in 1947). Here one of the batch – No 190 – is seen in Market Place passing in front of the National Provincial Bank; the bank building, latterly a branch – now closed – of NatWest, was built in the early twentieth century and is, at the time of writing, still vacant although planning permission has been granted for its conversion. *Harry Luff/Online Transport Archive*

Opposite above: **The first** new non-Utility trolleybuses acquired by Derby after the Second World War were thirty Sunbeam F4s fitted with Brush fifty-six-seat bodywork. Here No 202 is pictured at the Shelton Lock terminus of route 66. All were taken out of service between 1963 and 1967; of the two that survived into 1967, one – No 215 – was preserved on withdrawal. *J. Joyce/Online Transport Archive*

Opposite below: **During 1952** and 1953, Derby took delivery of a further batch of Sunbeam F4s; Nos 216-35 were fitted with Willowbrook sixty-seat bodywork and their arrival permitted the withdrawal of the last of the pre-war Guy BTXs. Seen here on Victoria Street outside the Spotted Horse pub, one of the batch – No 218 – loads passengers for a service on route 31 towards Osmaston Park Road. The 31 was destined to be one of the last trolleybus routes in Derby, being finally converted to bus operation in September 1967. All twenty of the batch survived into the final year of operation with No 224 being preserved on withdrawal. *Marcus Eavis/Online Transport Archive*

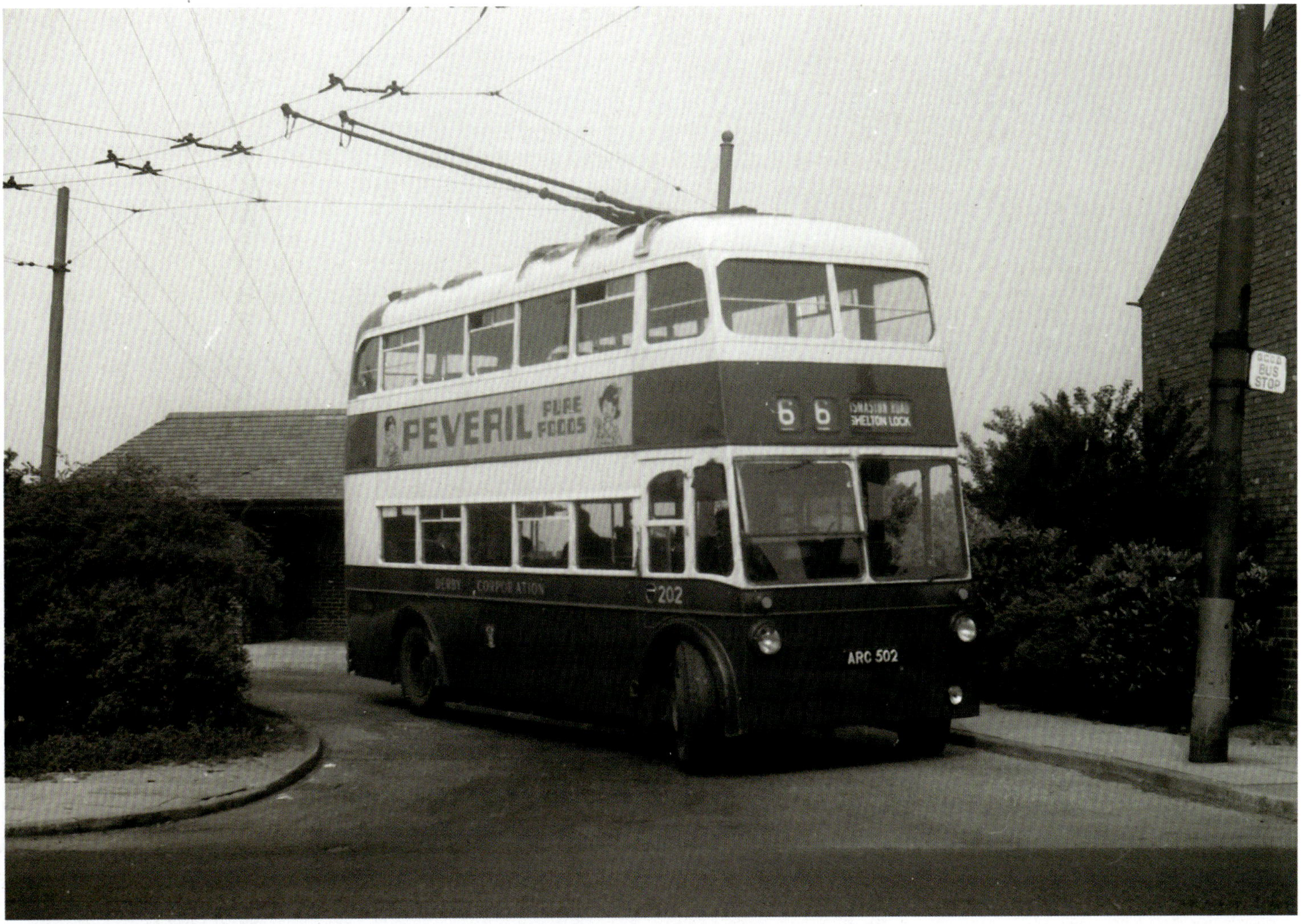
PEVERIL
PURE FOODS
SHELTON LOCK
DERBY CORPORATION
202
ARC 502
BUS STOP

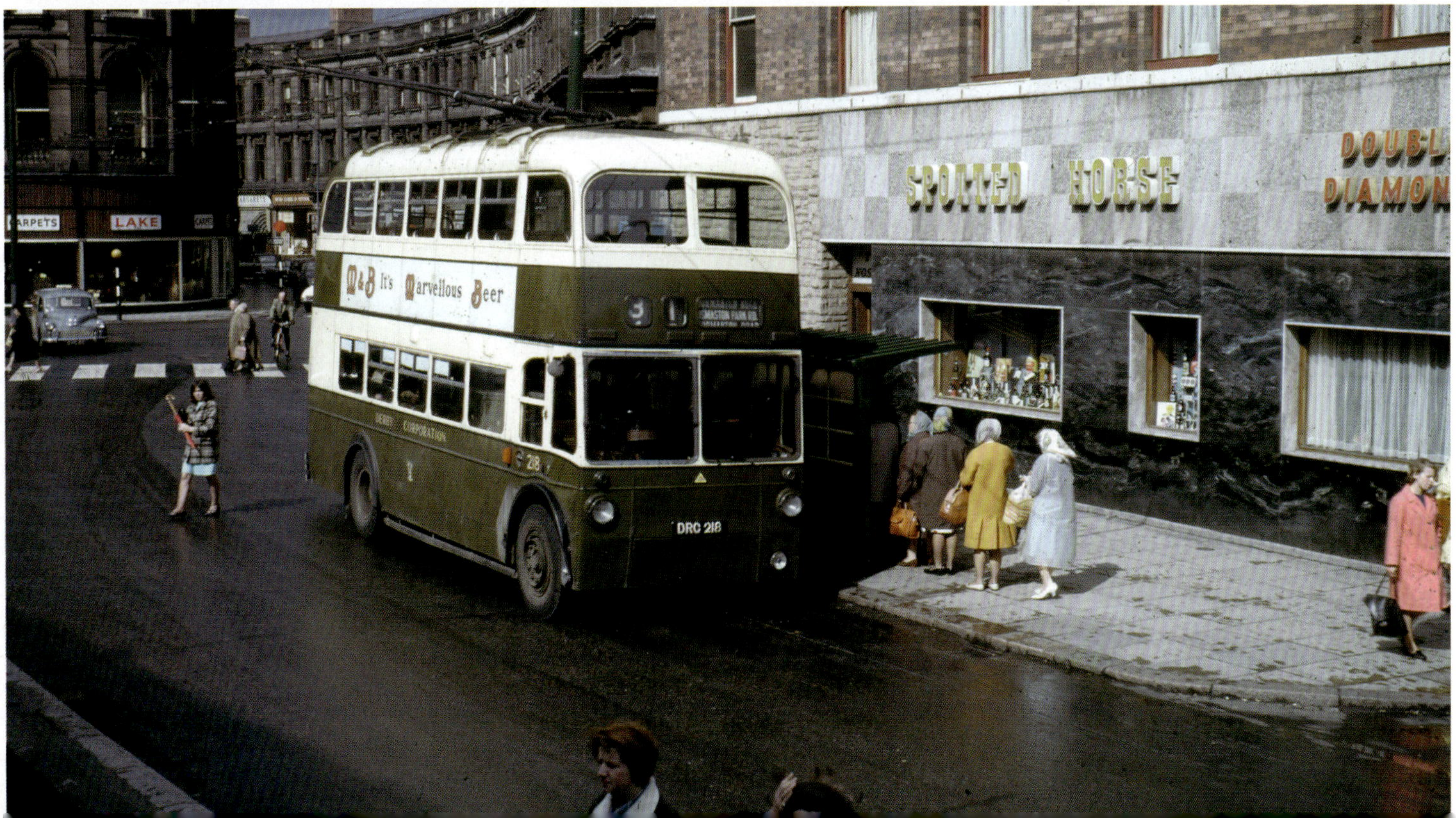
M&B It's Marvellous Beer
SPOTTED HORSE
LAKE
DERBY CORPORATION
218
DRC 218

Right: **On** 26 July 1953, the last route extension in Derby saw the 22 along Ashbourne Road extended from Prince Charles Avenue to Morden Green. On the opening day, the Southern Counties Touring Society had organised a tour of the system and took advantage of a trip over the new extension. One of the Sunbeam F4s delivered during 1952 and 1953 – Nos 219 – was used as the tour vehicle and is pictured here at the new terminus. *John Meredith/Online Transport Archive*

Below: **With** the famous Assembly Rooms forming the background – a building which was demolished (after a fire in 1963) towards the end of the trolleybus era with its façade being reconstructed at the National Tramway Museum – two of the last batch of trolleybuses – Nos 242 on route 88 to Sinfin Lane and 238 on route 60 to Shelton Lock – are seen in Market Place. The final eight trolleybuses purchased by Derby were Sunbeam F4As but time fitted with Roe-built sixty-five-seat bodywork. All survived into 1967 with No 237 eventually being preserved. *Marcus Eavis/Online Transport Archive*

Fleet number	Registration	Chassis	Body	New	Withdrawn	Notes
79-84	RC401-406	Guy BTX	Brush H56R	1932	1946-49	
85-92	RC544-551	Guy BTX	Dodson H56R	1932	1946-49	
93-98	RC793-798	Guy BTX	Dodson H56R	1932	1948-49	
99	RC799	Karrier-Clough	Dodson H56R	1932	1950	
100	RC800	Sunbeam MS2	Dodson H56R	1932	1950	
101	RC801	Ransomes	Ransomes H56R	1932	1950	
102-13	RC1102-1113	Guy BTX	Weymann H56R	1933	1946-50	
114	RC1414	Thornycroft HD	Brush H56R	1933	1950	
115-34	RC1615-1634	Guy BTX	Brush H56R	1933/34	1948-52	
135-44	RC2035-2038/ 2319-2144	Guy BTX	Brush H56R	1934	1948-52	
145-48	RC2645-2648	Guy BTX	Brush H56R	1935	1952	
149-58	R4349-4358	Guy BTX	Brush H56R	1936/37	1949-53	
159-64	RC6659-6664	Daimler CTM4	Brush H54R	1938	1959-60	
165-70	DY5113/5115/ 5123/5137/ 5140/5134	Guy BT	Ransomes B32C	1928-29	1942-45	Ex-Hastings 11,13, 21, 35, 38 and 57; acquired 1942. 167 and 170 never entered service
171 and 172	RC8471/72	Sunbeam W	Weymann H56R	1944	1964	172 preserved
173-75	RC8573-8575	Sunbeam W	PR H56R	1945	1963-64	175 preserved
176-85	R8876-8885	Sunbeam W	PR H56R	1946	1964-66	
186-96	ARC486-496	Sunbeam F4	Brush H56R	1948	1963-66	
197-215	ARC497-515	Sunbeam F4	Brush H56R	1949	1963-67	215 preserved
216-24	DRC216-224	Sunbeam F4	Willowbrook H60R	1952	1967	224 preserved
225-35	DRC225-235	Sunbeam F4	Willowbrook H60R	1953	1967	
236-43	SCH236-243	Sunbeam F4A	Roe H65R	1960	1967	237 preserved

Route number	From	To	Date Opened	Date Closed	Notes
N/A	London Road	Osmaston Road	April 1958	9 September 1967	Ascot Drive section; only used for specials and depot workings; workshops opened June 1949; first trolleybuses allocated to depot September 1949; all trolleybuses allocated from February 1961
11	Midland station	Kedleston Road (Allestree Lane)	28 April 1935	11 February 1967	Linked with Harvey Road from 26 July 1964
22	Midland station	Ashbourne Road (Kingsway)	31 December 1933	9 September 1967	Linked with Osmaston Park Road from 26 July 1964
22	Ashbourne Road (Kingsway)	Prince Charles Avenue	8 June 1952	9 September 1967	Linked with Osmaston Park Road from 26 July 1964
22	Prince Charles Avenue	Morden Green	26 July 1953	9 September 1967	Linked with Osmaston Park Road from 26 July 1964
30	Cavendish Hotel (Normanton)	Browning Circle	30 January 1935	30 January 1960	Service 34 extended and renumbered; linked with Uttoxeter Road service
31	Victoria Street	Osmaston Park Road (via The Vulcan and Barracks)	13 November 1932	9 September 1967	Linked with route 41 to form a circular route; route number switched to 41 for inbound journey at The Mitre; 39 was short working to Victory Road
33	Victoria Street	Midland station	18 March 1934	26 November 1966	Cavendish Hotel (Normanton) circle; 34 was Victoria Street to Cavendish only; limited services into spring 1967 to cover motorbus duties if necessary
41	Market Place	Harvey Road (via Alvaston)	29 November 1936	9 September 1967	Linked with route 31 to form a circular route; route number switched to 31 for inbound journey at The Mitre
43	Market Place	Wyndham Street	24 July 1932	1 January 1966	

Route number	From	To	Date Opened	Date Closed	Notes
43 (renumbered 57 from 3 October 1964)	Market Place	Duffield Road (Broadway)	11 July 1937	3 October 1964	Linked with Wyndham Street service from opening; renumbered when linked with Burton Road route on 3 October 1964
43 (renumbered 57 from 3 October 1964)	Duffield Road (Broadway)	King's Croft	14 September 1947	3 October 1964	Renumbered when linked with Burton Road route on 3 October 1964
44 (renumbered 57 by October 1950)	Market Place	Harvey Road (via Alvaston)	13 November 1932	By 1955	
55	Victoria Street	Burton Road	13 August 1933	3 October 1964	
55	Victoria Street	Uttoxeter Road	13 August 1933	26 November 1966	Limited services into spring 1967 to cover motorbus duties if necessary; renumbered 54 when linked with Normanton routes via Victoria Street in 1950s
60	Nottingham Road	Chaddesden Park Road	29 November 1936	11 June 1950	Route 60 previously used for service linking Market Place with Pear Tree; overhead retained until 1962 for specials
60	Allenton	Shelton Lock	6 November 1938	9 September 1967	Terminated at Market Place following withdrawal of Nottingham Road service on 10 November 1962
66	Market Place	Allenton (Osmaston Road)	13 November 1932	9 September 1967	Through service to Nottingham Road reinstated 13 November 1932; renumbered 60 and terminated at Market Place following withdrawal of Nottingham Road service on 10 November 1962
66	Market Place	Nottingham Road	10 January 1932	10 November 1962	Final services over Chaddesden Park Road as well
88	Barracks	Sinfin Lane	30 August 1943	1 January 1966	Limited services to 3 April 1966 to cover motorbus duties if necessary

GRIMSBY-CLEETHORPES

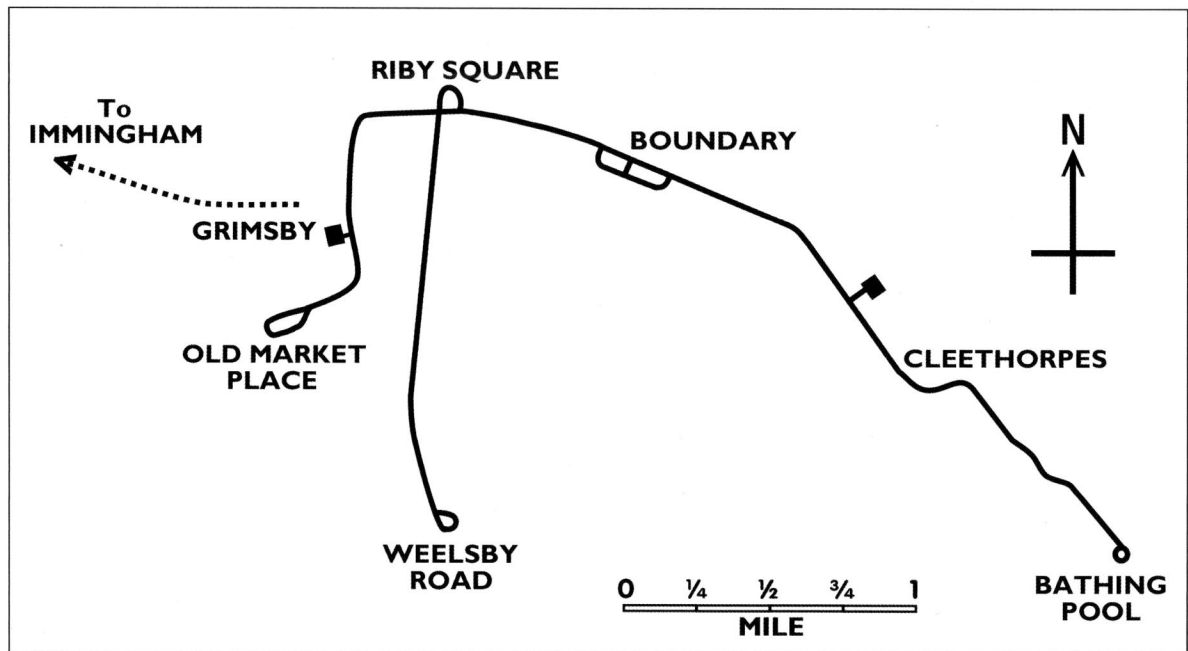

The origins of public transport provision in Grimsby and Cleethorpes lay with the Great Grimsby Street Tramways Co (a subsidiary of the Provincial Tramways Co). This company introduced horse trams to the district on 4 June 1881 with electric trams operating from 7 December 1901.

Under the terms of the Tramways Act of 1870 and the Grimsby Corporation Act of 1921, Grimsby Corporation served notice on the company on 18 July 1921 of its intention to take-over the company's assets within its boundaries on 21 July 1922. However, negotiations for the take-over at an agreed price took some time and it was not until 6 April 1925 that the take-over was completed. This meant that the company's activities were now restricted to operation within the Cleethorpes area only.

The tramway at Grimsby was, however, in a poor condition; in particular the track south from Riby Square to Hainton Avenue required replacement. At a meeting on 5 June 1925, at which the costs for renewing the tram track or replacing it with trolleybuses – the cheaper option – were presented, it was decided to replace the trams with trolleybuses. The last trams operated on the route on 2 October 1926 with trolleybuses being introduced the following day with the route extended to Weelsby Road. The initial fleet comprised five single-deckers supplied by Garrett but the success of the operation resulted in two further Garretts being acquired the following year. In order to gain access to the corporation's depot on Victoria Street, the trolleybuses made use of a skate and the surviving tram track and overhead.

Grimsby's first trolleybuses were seven Garrett Ss fitted with Roe thirty-six-seat bodywork; Nos 1-5 were delivered during 1926 for the opening of the initial route in October that year, whilst Nos 6 and 7 were delivered the following year. No 1 – illustrated here – was the first of the septet to be withdrawn – during 1939 – but the last of the type remained in service until 1946. *D.W.K. Jones Collection/ Online Transport Archive*

The success of the new route encouraged the corporation to consider a number of extensions and an Act – the Grimsby Corporation Act – received the Royal Assent on 29 July 1927 to permit the replacement of the remaining tramways by trolleybuses, the extension of a number of trolleybus extensions and the introduction of motorbus services. In the event, the proposed trolleybus extensions were not progressed, and the corporation opted to use motorbuses as a cheaper alternative.

There the story of trolleybus operation in north Lincolnshire rested for almost a decade. The company and Grimsby Corporation continued to operate the tramway service from Old Market Place, Grimsby, or Riby Square via the borough boundary at Park Street through to Kingsway in Cleethorpes but Cleethorpes UDC was already starting to look to the future. The Cleethorpes Urban District Council Act, which received the Royal Assent on 3 August 1928, stated that it was 'An Act to make provision for the working of tramways and trolley vehicles by the urban district council of Cleethorpes to empower the Council to run omnibuses to confer further powers on them in regard to the supply of electricity and the management of public walks and pleasure grounds to authorise them to purchase the Cleethorpes Pier and Gardens and to make further and better provision for the health[,] local government[,] finance and improvement of their district and for other purposes.'

Grimsby Corporation agreed in 1932 that, should the section in Cleethorpes be converted to trolleybus operation, it would similarly convert the section from Market Square to the boundary. However, nothing progressed until the mid-1930s, when, in furtherance of the scheme, Grimsby ordered ten double-deck trolleybuses from AEC and Cleethorpes formally took over the ownership of its section of tramway from the company – for £50,000 – on 15 July 1937. The Ministry of Transport issued a Provisional Order under the 1928 Act in early 1937 – it was formally presented on 28 April 1937 – and work progressed on the erection of the overhead in Cleethorpes.

In Grimsby, the section of tramway from Old Market Place to Park Street, where a loop was installed, was converted to trolleybus operation on 22 November 1936, although corporation and Cleethorpes trams continued to operate the through service from Riby Square to Kingsway until 17 July 1937, when the last trams operated. On 18 July 1937, the through trolleybus service was introduced. The trolleybuses were extended slightly in Cleethorpes to terminate in a loop at the Bathing Pool.

As a seaside resort, Cleethorpes witnessed a decline in traffic during the Second World War; as a result, four of the thirteen AECs that it had purchased to operate its services were sold to Nottingham in 1940. These were replaced post-war by the purchase of six new vehicles in 1950 and 1951; Cleethorpes Nos 59-64 were to prove the last new trolleybuses acquired by either Cleethorpes or Grimsby and all were sold eventually to Walsall following the system's conversion in 1960.

Grimsby No 12 – seen here in Victoria Street South on 22 August 1951 – was one of ten AEC 663Ts supplied with Roe-built centre-entrance bodywork in 1936. These were acquired to permit the introduction of the service from the Market Place in Grimsby to the borough boundary on 22 November 1936. Following the conversion of the Cleethorpes tram route, the trolleybus service was extended through to the Bathing Pool at Cleethorpes on 18 July 1937. Of the ten AECs that Grimsby acquired in 1936, four – Nos 11, 14 16 and 17 – passed to the joint undertaking when it was created on 1 January 1957. The other five, including No 12, were withdrawn in 1955 following the conversion of the route from Riby Square to Weelsby Road. *C. Carter/Online Transport Archive*

Although Grimsby acquired nine new vehicles between 1944 and 1947 and, post-war, there were proposals to extend the system, the latter were not constructed and, by the early 1950s, the trolleybus was not favoured. In mid-1955 the Weelsby Road service was temporarily converted to motorbus operation; this was made permanent on 1 October the same year and resulted in the first withdrawals of the pre-war AECs.

The final phase in the story of the system came on 1 January 1957 when the long-mooted creation of Grimsby-Cleethorpes Transport joint committee took place. A new livery was adopted – blue and cream – with thirteen trolleybuses from Grimsby and eleven from Cleethorpes being transferred; however, five of these were to be withdrawn by the end of the year, with a further four following in 1958 and three in 1959.

One of the first actions of the new committee was to close the Cleethorpes depot at Pelham Road on 2 March 1957; thereafter all trolleybus services were operated from Victoria Street. In September 1958, Sunday services ceased and, in October 1959, a report advocating conversion was prepared. When the original joint committee was set up two years earlier, it had been agreed that both councils had to agree before the trolleybus service could be converted; during November 1959 both councils acquiesced. The final conversion took place on 4 June 1960.

Of the trolleybuses that survived into 1960, the six post-war Cleethorpes vehicles were sold to Walsall where three underwent significant rebuilding whilst five of the Grimsby post-war Karrier Ws were sold to Bradford. Whilst the latter were allocated fleet numbers and would probably have been part of the rebodying programme had Bradford's policy not changed, in the event none entered service in the West Riding.

Two of the fleet survive in preservation, both ex-Cleethorpes: No 154 was one of the pre-war AEC 661Ts which was rescued in 1968 having spent a decade in a scrapyard whilst No 159 was one of the 1950 BUTs sold to Walsall and the only one of the quartet not rebuilt.

On 23 July 1950 Grimsby No 2 is seen at the Grimsby station terminus. No 2 was one of three Karrier Ws fitted with Roe Utility bodywork that were supplied to the corporation in 1944. All three passed to the joint committee on 1 January 1957 and retained their utility bodies right through until withdrawal in 1958. *Peter N. Williams/Online Transport Archive*

Right: **The last** new trolleybuses acquired by Grimsby Corporation were six Karrier Ws – Nos 19-24 – that were supplied during 1946 and 1947. Fitted with Roe bodywork all six passed to the joint committee in 1957 but two – Nos 20 and 23 – were withdrawn in 1959. The remaining four, withdrawn in June 1960, were all sold to Bradford along with No 20. Allocated the fleet numbers 822-25/27 and had Bradford's policy not been reversed, these would have been rebodied before re-entering service; as it was, however, they never operated again and were sold for scrap in November 1962. *Harry Luff/Online Transport Archive*

Below: **On 22 August** 1951, Cleethorpes No 52 is pictured in Grimsby. This was one of a batch of ten – Nos 50-59 – AEC 661Ts fitted with Park Royal bodywork that Cleethorpes acquired in 1937 for the conversion of its only tram route – that from the borough boundary with Grimsby to the Bathing Pool – on 18 July 1937 (the beginning of the joint service between the two towns). Of the 10, one – No 59 – was sold to Nottingham Corporation in 1940 with a further six being withdrawn between 1950 and 1954. Three – Nos 54, 55 and 58 – passed to the joint committee on 1 January 1957 with all three being withdrawn by the end of 1959. No 154 (ex-Cleethorpes No 54) is preserved.
C. Carter/Online Transport Archive

In 1950 four BUT 9611Ts – Nos 59-62 – fitted with NCB bodywork were acquired by Cleethorpes; these took the fleet numbers of four trolleybuses sold to Nottingham in 1940. No 61 is pictured here turning at the system's southern loop at the Bathing Pool, Cleethorpes. Following the conversion of the final trolleybus route on 5 June 1960, all four were sold to Walsall Corporation. Subsequent to the conversion of the Walsall system in 1970, No 159 (the only one not rebuilt in the West Midlands) was preserved. *Harry Luff/Online Transport Archive*

Also seen at the Bathing Pool loop is Cleethorpes No 63; this was one of two Crossley Empire trolleybuses that were fitted with Roe bodywork. New in 1951, Nos 63 and 64 – later joint committee Nos 163 and 164 – were the last new trolleybuses to be supplied to either Grimsby or Cleethorpes. The two vehicles were also sold to Walsall Corporation in 1960. *Harry Luff/Online Transport Archive*

Although the idea of combining the Grimsby and Cleethorpes operations together had been discussed for some years, it was not to take place until 1 January 1957 when a new joint committee was established. Pictured in the new livery with the new operator's name prominently displayed is the second of the Cleethorpes Crossleys – No 164. The surviving ex-Grimsby trolleybuses retained their original fleet numbers whilst those from Cleethorpes were renumbered by adding 100 to the original. It was agreed that conversion of the system to bus operation would only take place if both councils agreed; unity was achieved following a report in November 1959 and the through service was converted on 5 June 1960. *Harry Luff/Online Transport Archive*

Grimsby Fleet number	Registration	Chassis	Body	New	Withdrawn	Notes
1-5 (3 renumbered 5 in 1944)	EE6461-6465	Garrett O	Roe B36C	1926	1939-45	
6-7	EE7097-7098	Garrett O	Roe B36C	1927	1944-46	
8-12, 14-18	JV5001-5005/ 5007-5010/5006	AEC 663T	Roe H56C	1936	1955*	* 8-10, 12, 15 and 18; 11, 14, 16 and 17 passed to the joint committee in 1957
1-3	JV8701-8703	Karrier W	PR H56R	1944	N/A	Passed to the joint committee in 1957
19-24	AEE22-27	Karrier W	Roe H56R	1946-47	N/A	Passed to the joint committee in 1957

Cleethorpes Fleet number	Registration	Chassis	Body	New	Withdrawn	Notes
50-59	FW8986-8995	AEC 661T	PR H56R	1937	1940-54*	59 sold to Nottingham 1940; * all except 54, 55 and 58, which passed to the joint committee in 1957
60-62	AFU153-155	AEC 661T	PR H56R	1938	1940	Sold to Nottingham 1940
59-62	GFU692-695	BUT 9611T	NCB H54R	1950	N/A	Passed to the joint committee in 1957
63-64	HBE541-542	Crossley TDD42/3	Roe H54R	1951	N/A	Passed to the joint committee in 1957

Grimsby-Cleethorpes Fleet number	Registration	Chassis	Body	New	Withdrawn	Notes
1-3	JV8701-8703	Karrier W	PR H56R	N/A	1958	Ex-Grimsby 1-3
11, 14, 16 and 17	JV5004/5007/5009/5010	AEC 663T	Roe H56C	N/A	1957	Ex-Grimsby 11, 14, 16 and 17
19-24	AEE22-27	Karrier W	Roe H56R	N/A	1959-60	Ex-Grimsby 19-24; 19-22 and 24 sold to Bradford
154, 155 and 158	FW8990/8991/8994	AEC 661T	PR H56R	N/A	1957-59	Ex-Cleethorpes 54, 55 and 58; 154 preserved
159-62	GFU692-695	BUT 9611T	NCB H54R	N/A	1960	Ex-Cleethorpes 59-62; sold to Walsall; 159 preserved
163 and 164	HBE541-542	Crossley TDD42/3	Roe H54R	N/A	1960	Ex-Cleethorpes 63 and 64; sold to Walsall

Route number	From	To	Date Opened	Date Closed	Notes
10	Riby Square	Weelsby Road	3 October 1926	1 October 1955 (date at which the temporary conversion of the route was made permanent)	Grimsby Corporation service
11	Old Market Place	Cleethorpes boundary	22 November 1936	4 June 1960	Grimsby Corporation service
11	Cleethorpes boundary	Bathing Pool	18 July 1937	4 June 1960	Cleethorpes Corporation service; 12 was a short working from Riby Square to High Cliff; 11 also used for joint service from Old Market Place to Bathing Pool

Pictured at the Old Market Place on 27 August 1951 is Grimsby No 11; this was one of four of the batch – the others being Nos 14, 16 and 17 – that passed to the joint committee in 1957. However, they were not to survive long, all being withdrawn by the end of that year. *C. Carter/Online Transport Archive*

There were a number of railway level crossings in the Grimsby area; one of them with Cleethorpes Road was immediately to the north of Grimsby Dock station. Seen heading east over the crossing in early 1956 is Cleethorpes No 62. This was the last of the batch of four BUT 9611Ts that was new in 1950. Passing to the joint committee in 1957 and being renumbered 162, this was one of six ex-Cleethorpes trolleybuses sold to Walsall Corporation in 1960. Today this scene is radically different with the level crossing now been replaced by a road overbridge. *Phil Tatt/Online Transport Archive*

IPSWICH

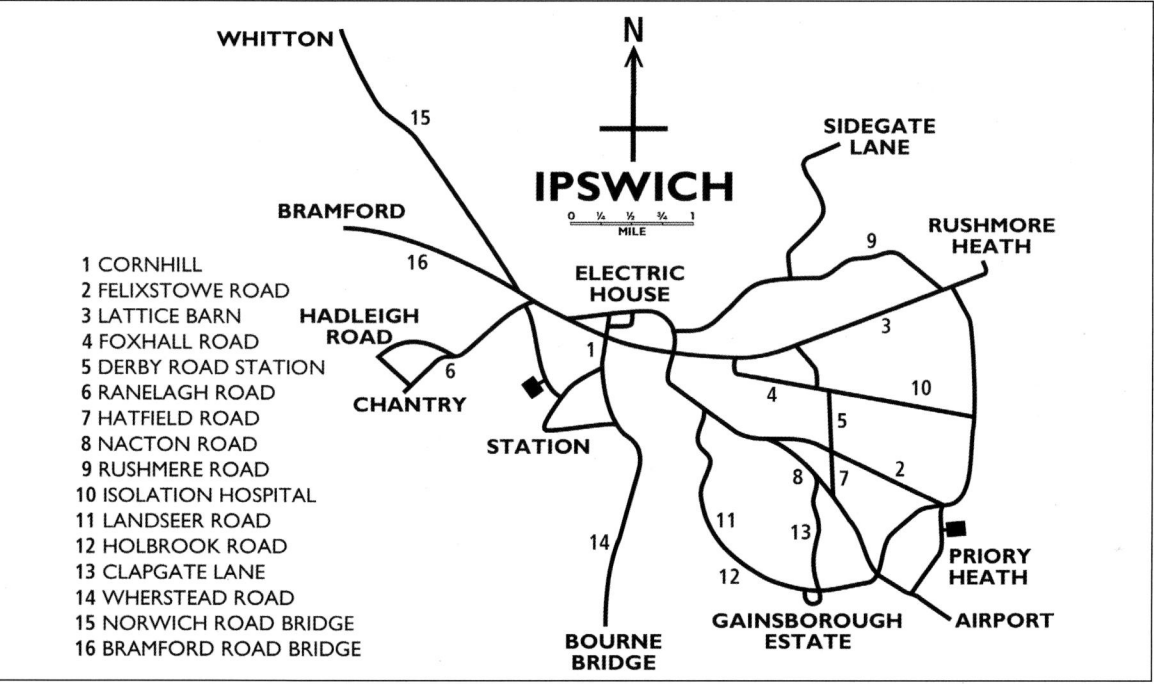

There were a handful of British operators that relied on trolleybuses to provide, for a period, their entire fleet; Darlington was one example, Ipswich was another. With the benefit of hindsight, this was both a strength, when the trolleybus was in the ascendancy, and a weakness when fashions changed and when there was a need to extend the system beyond the traditional core routes.

From November 1903, Ipswich Corporation developed an electric tramway system; at its peak, the 3ft 6in gauge network extended over almost eleven route miles. As elsewhere, the First World War resulted in a deterioration in the condition of the tram track and, although some track was relayed post-war, in 1923 the future of the system came under consideration. It was decided to seek powers to abandon the tramway system and replace it with trolleybuses. Although powers to undertake this were not obtained until the Ipswich Corporation Act 1925 received the Royal Assent on 7 August 1925, work on the installation of an experimental route – modifying the existing tramway overhead on the ¾-mile section from Cornhill to the railway station – was undertaken in 1923 and, following the arrival of three single-deckers on loan from Railless Ltd, services were introduced on 2 September 1923, resulting in the cessation of tram operation on this section and that along Mill Street and Portman Road.

Initially neither the surviving trams nor the new trolleybuses were popular, with the motorbus seeming to be preferred as a means of tramway replacement. However, the trolleybus was to be the choice, after a referendum of ratepayers in early 1925 and, after

The first three Ipswich trolleybuses – Nos 1-3 – were all supplied by Railless and fitted with Short single-deck bodies. New in 1923, the trio were to survive until withdrawal between 1933 and 1935. Here, No 1 is pictured outside the Station Hotel. *Barry Cross Collection/Online Transport Archive*

Between 1926 and 1930, Ipswich was supplied with twenty-four single-deck trolleybuses by the locally-based Ransomes, Sims & Jefferies; these were all fitted with the same manufacturer's bodywork and were delivered to allow the opening of the routes permitted under the Ipswich Corporation Act of 1925. This posed view taken in 1926 shows the first fifteen delivered – Nos 6-20 – when new. No 9, which is seen at the front of the impressive line-up, was eventually to be preserved and is part of the collection at the Ipswich Transport Museum. Of the fifteen, eight were withdrawn before the Second World War, four during 1940, with the remainder succumbing between 1945 and 1951; No 9 was taken out of service in 1949. *J. Joyce Collection/Online Transport Archive*

passage of the 1925 Act, the conversion progressed rapidly – indeed, the first conversion took place on the route to Bourne Bridge on 17 July 1925 prior to the passing of the legislation. The remaining tram routes were all converted within three months during 1926. The Royal Oak route, extended along Felixstowe Road, was the first on 27 May; this was followed on 9 June by the conversion of the routes to Lattice Barn and Derby Road station. Finally, on 26 July, the last trams operated on the Whitton and Bramford routes; trolleybuses were introduced to both services the following day. For these new services, a further thirty single-deck trolleybuses – split equally between two Suffolk-based manufacturers Richard Garrett & Sons Ltd of Leiston and Ransomes, Sims & Jefferies Ltd of Ipswich – were delivered during 1926. Apart from one additional Garrett supplied in 1931, all the remaining vehicles delivered before 1940 were all supplied by Ransomes, Sims & Jefferies. The connection was possibly not harmed by the fact that the Ipswich general manager until 1925, when he was succeeded by A.S. Black, was W.F. Ayton who had become general manager at Ransomes.

With the original tramway routes now replaced and extended, further expansion of the trolleybus network took place with the Derby Road station service extended to Spring Road on 22 December 1926, to Heath Lane on 29 March 1927 and to Kings Way (via Hatfield Road, Nacton Road and Landseer Road to create a circular service with route 4) on 18 March 1928. On 29 March 1927 the first section of the London Road route to Ranelegh Road opened.

During the 1930s, three pieces of legislation – the Ipswich Corporation (Trolley Vehicles) Provisional Order Act 1931, Ipswich Corporation (Trolley Vehicles) Provisional Order Act 1935 and the Ipswich Corporation (Trolley Vehicles) Provisional Order Act 1938 were given the Royal Assent on 21 May 1931, 27 May 1935 and 24 May 1938 respectively – gave the corporation powers to undertake the considerable expansion of the system. Between 28 July 1931 and 26 February 1940 no fewer than eleven extensions were opened – as detailed in the table – although the opening of the link between Priory Heath and Felixstowe Road via Lindbergh Road resulted in the first abandonment when services over the parallel section via Kings Way and Rands Way were abandoned without replacement on 23 April 1939. The expansion of the network required the construction of a new depot and works to supplement the existing depot on Constantine Road; the new facility – at Priory Heath – opened on 6 March 1937.

Although there were no extensions opened during the war, the fleet was strengthened by the acquisition of two batches of Utility-bodied Karrier Ws; this permitted the withdrawal of more of the older single-deck trolleybuses with the result that the fleet in 1946 comprised fifty-seven double-deckers and seventeen single-deckers operating over a network that comprised almost 23½ route miles. Between 1945 and 1949 four further extensions opened. The first of these – on 17 December 1945 – saw services run from Nacton Road to the Gainsborough Estate via Clapgate Lane; this was followed in 1947 by the section from Woodbridge Road to a new terminus at Sidegate Lane. On 17 August 1947 the Nacton Road service was extended to the Airport. Finally, on 10 July 1949, a link between Electric House and Cornhill along Lloyds Avenue was opened.

Nos 37-41 were new during 1928 and 1929; here, No 38, is pictured on Lloyds Avenue on 7 August 1950. Of this batch of five, all were withdrawn between 1950 and 1953.
C. Carter/Online Transport Archive

Between 1948 and 1950, the corporation took delivery of a further twenty-four new double-deckers; the batch of twelve delivered in 1950 proved to be the last new trolleybuses acquired. The system had now reached its apogee with eighty-eight trolleybuses operating over 25½ route miles. In April 1950, the new Cliff Quay power station – designed to replace the original corporation power station at Constantine Road – was officially opened; however, by this date the electricity supply industry had been nationalised thus breaking the link between the transport department and the electricity supplier.

The last batch of single-deckers supplied by RS&J was represented by Nos 42-44 that were new in 1930. No 43 is pictured here at the Adair Road teminus prior to heading back towards the centre and station. The pub in the background was one of a number built by the local brewery Tollemache during the 1930s that were nicknamed 'Tolly Follies'. It survived as a pub until 1994 and was demolished a decade later. The Bramford route was converted to bus operation in September 1953 – the first route to succumb – and this resulted in the demise of the majority of the surviving single-deckers, including No 43. No 44, which was to survive until 1955, was preserved by the Science Museum and was based at the museum's Wroughton store, but is now being transferred to the Ipswich Transport Museum.
Harry Luff/Online Transport Archive

As elsewhere, new housing estates had been developed beyond the existing trolleybus termini and the corporation decided that these would be served by motorbus rather than trolleybus. As a result, on 4 May 1950, Ipswich introduced its first motorbuses on a service to the Whitehouse Estate; almost fifty years of complete operation by electric traction had come to an end. It was not until 6 September 1953, however, that the first trolleybus-to-motorbus conversion was undertaken (although the eastern circular route had been abandoned without replacement in 1951); this was the Bramford Road service where a low railway bridge had precluded the operation of double-deckers. Its conversion permitted the withdrawal of most of the surviving single-deckers; the last were finally taken out of service in 1955 with No 44 preserved (initially by the Science Museum but to be transferred to the Ipswich Transport Museum).

The actual conversion of the remaining network was complex as often limited services persisted but gradually, over ten years, the trolleybus gradually disappeared from Ipswich's streets. The next conversion – on 22 May 1954 – was the Bourne Bridge route; this was followed on 28 July 1956 by the service along London Road to Chantry Park and the section along St Johns Road via Derby Road station and Hatfield Road that linked the Rushmere Heath and Priory Heath routes. The service along Foxhall Road to Foxhall Circus was

Between 1933 and 1936, Ipswich acquired twenty-two double-deck trolleybuses from Ransomes, Sims & Jefferies; Nos 46-67 were fitted with the same manufacturer's forty-eight-seat bodywork typified by No 62 pictured here and were the first double-deckers delivered to the corporation. During 1949 and 1950 Nos 46-67 were reseated to provide an additional two seats on the lower deck. All twenty-two were withdrawn between 1950 and 1955. No 46 survives in preservation and awaits restoration at the Ipswich Transport Museum. *Harry Luff/Online Transport Archive*

converted on 31 May 1958 followed by those to Bixley Road and Heath Road on 30 May 1959 and to Colchester Road and Sidegate Lane on 30 May 1959 and 1 October 1959 respectively.

The penultimate stage in the programme saw the conversion of the routes to Whitton and to Rushmere Heath succumb on 28 April 1962. This left the complex network of routes serving the south-east of the town – the Airport, Priory Heath and the Gainsborough Estate via either Clapgate Land or Landseer Road – operational; these were converted on 23 August 1963. The last service was operated by No 114 with its lower-deck side panels crudely painted with 'RIP' and a notice stating 'This is DEFINITELY the last trolleybus'. There was no official closure ceremony.

Although the Ipswich system had closed, eight of the last batch – Nos 119-26 – were sold for further service to Walsall with No 126 being subsequently preserved following withdrawal in the West Midlands. Apart from this and No 44, five other Ipswich trolleybuses also survive in preservation (along with the chassis of two others). This includes one of the original trio, No 2, that was sold in 1934 and used as a caravan; rescued in 1977 it is now based at the Ipswich Transport Museum along with Nos 9, 16 (chassis only), 46 and 105, with No 105 now restored to a fully operational condition. No 26 also survives at the Long Shop Museum at Leiston.

Pictured having just crossed over the River Orwell on Princess Street and about to turn into Burrell Road is No 76; it is displaying 'Private' in the destination box as it was being employed on an enthusiasts' tour. No 76 was one of eighteen – Nos 68-85 – vehicles supplied during 1937 and 1938. Again the chasses were produced by Ransomes, Sims & Jefferies but the forty-eight-seat bodies were manufactured by the Wigan-based Massey Brothers. All were reseated to fifty-four during the period 1949 to 1954 and all were withdrawn between 1955 and 1959. When No 81 was withdrawn on 22 March 1958, it was the last Ransomes, Sims & Jefferies-built trolleybus still operational in Britain. *Frank Hunt/LRTA (London Area) Collection/Online Transport Archive*

70 • BRITISH TROLLEYBUS SYSTEMS – WALES, MIDLANDS AND EAST ANGLIA

Right: **In 1940,** the corporation took delivery of its sixty-sixth and last trolleybus supplied by Ransomes, Sims & Jefferies. This was also the last trolleybus supplied by the manufacturer to any UK trolleybus operator although the company did continue to produce vehicles for the export market. The last order – in 1948 – was a batch sent to Drammen in Norway. Ipswich's last RS&J – No 86 – was fitted with a body supplied by Massey and remained in service until 1958. *J. Joyce/Online Transport Archive*

Below: **On 16 March** 1958 No 89 – one of four Karrier Ws fitted with Weymann Utility fifty-six-seat bodywork that were new in 1944 – is seen on Crown Street, in the company of Sunbeam No 121 and AEC Monarch tower wagon PV8580. By this date, the four Karriers were approaching the end of their life; all were withdrawn during 1958. *John Meredith/Online Transport Archive*

In 1945, Ipswich took delivery of a second batch of Utility-bodied Karrier Ws; Nos 91-102 were fitted with bodywork supplied, this time, by Park Royal. The new vehicles were essential as the system was to see the opening of a number of post-war extensions, the first of which – to Clapgate Lane – was introduced on 17 December 1945. Here No 100 is seen at Electric House in Tower Street on 16 March 1958. All twelve were taken out of service during 1960 and 1961. *John Meredith/Online Transport Archive*

Ipswich's third and final batch of Karrier Ws was Nos 103-08, which were new during 1948. Fitted with Park Royal bodywork, all six were eventually withdrawn between 1961 and 1963. Here No 105 – which following withdrawal in 1962 was subsequently to be preserved – stands in front of the Cricketers Hotel on Crown Street with a service towards Rushmere Heath. One of the batch, No 105, is now fully restored to operational condition at the Ipswich Transport Museum. *J. Joyce/Online Transport Archive*

Alongside the six Karrier Ws delivered during 1948, there were a further six Karriers – Nos 109-14 – that were F4s also fitted with Park Royal fifty-six-seat bodywork in 1949. Typical of the batch was No 113, which is seen here making use of the loop at the Rushmere Heath terminus, situated at the junction of Woodbridge Road East and Playford Road, with a service destined ultimately for Whitton. With the sale of the bulk of the 1950 batch of Sunbeam F4s to Walsall, it was the surviving members of the two Karrier batches delivered in the late 1940s that were to become the last trolleybuses to operate in Ipswich; one of F4s – No 114 – was destined to be Ipswich's last trolleybus on 23 August 1963 when it operated with bunting and the legend 'RIP' crudely painted on its lower-deck side panels. *Marcus Eavis/Online Transport Archive*

One of the last batch of trolleybuses acquired by Ipswich – No 122 – is pictured on the north side of the Electric House terminus prior to heading eastbound with a service to Priory Heath via St Johns Road. No 122 was one of twelve Sunbeam F4s fitted with Park Royal bodywork supplied in 1950; all were withdrawn during the final run down of the system during 1962 and 1963. After withdrawal, eight were sold to Walsall Corporation with No 125 being preserved at the Ipswich Transport Museum following withdrawal in the West Midlands. *Marcus Eavis/Online Transport Archive*

Fleet number	Registration	Chassis	Body	New	Withdrawn	Notes
1-3	DX3970/3988/3906	Railless	Short B30F	1923	1932-34	No 2 preserved
4	DX4648	RS&J	RS&J B30F	1924	1934	
5	DX5217	Tilling-Stevens	RS&J B30F	1925	1934	
6	DX5409	RS&J C	RS&J B30F	1925	1926	On loan from RS&J
6-20	DX5622/5608-5621	RS&J D	RS&J B30D	1926	1937-51	9 and 16 (chassis only) preserved
21-35	DX5626/5623-5625/5628/5629/5627/5630-5632/5634/5633/5635-5637	Garrett O	Strachan & Brown B30D	1926	1937-49	26 and chassis of 29 preserved
36	DX6014	RS&J D	RS&J B34D	1928	1940	
37-41	DX7620/7633/7651/7668/7683	RS&J D	RS&J B30D	1928/29	1950-53	
42-44	DX8869-8871	RS&J	RS&J B30D	1930	1953-55	44 preserved
45	DX9710	Garrett O	Garrett B31C	1931	1937	
46-49	PV817-820	RS&J	RS&J H48R (reseated to H50R in 1949-50)	1933	1951-52	46 preserved
50-59	PV1253-1256/1350-1355	RS&J	RS&J H48R (majority reseated to H50R)	1934	1952-54	
60-67	PV272-2734	RS&J	RS&J H48R (reseated to H50R in 1949-50)	1936	1950-55	
68-79	PV4061-4066/4540-4545	RS&J	Massey H48R (reseated to H54R in 1949-54)	1937	1955-58	
80-85	PV4788-4793	RS&J	Massey H48R (reseated to H54R in 1950-54)	1938	1956-59	
86	PV6426	RS&J	Massey H48R (reseated to H54R in 1949)	1940	1959	
87-90	PV6875-6878	Karrier W	Weymann UH56R	1944	1958	
91-102	PV6891-6896/6950-6955	Karrier W	PR UH56R	1945	1960-61	
103-08	PV8268-8273	Karrier W	PR H56R	1948	1961-63	105 preserved
109-14	PV8866-8871	Karrier F4	PR H56R	1949	1963	
115-26	ADX185-196	Sunbeam F4	PR H56R	1950	1962-63	119-26 sold to Walsall 1962; 126 preserved

Route number	From	To	Date Opened	Date Closed	Notes
X	Cornhill	Railway station	2 September 1923	July 1956	Peak, specials and depot use continued until April 1962
1	Cornhill	Bourne Bridge	17 July 1925	22 May 1954	1A was short working to Tyler Street 8 August 1933
4	Cornhill	Felixstowe Road (Kingsway)	27 May 1926	23 August 1963	Section from Felixstowe Road along Kings Way closed 23 April 1939; terminus thereafter St Augustine's church
3	Spring Road	Lattice Barn	9 June 1926	28 April 1963	
2	Spring Road	Derby Road station	9 June 1926	23 August 1963	
9	Cornhill	Whitton (Maypole Inn)	27 July 1926	28 April 1962	9A was short working to Cromer Road 8 August 1933
8	Cornhill	Bramford (Adair Road)	27 July 1926	6 September 1953	8A was short working to Kingston Road (opened 14 May 1950); low railway bridge beyond Kingston Road precluded the us of double-deckers through to Bramford
5	Spring Road	Derby Road station	22 December 1926	31 May 1958	
5	Derby Road station	Heath Lane	29 March 1927	31 May 1958	
7A	Barrack Corner (London Road)	Ranelagh Road	29 March 1927	29 July 1956	
2/2A	Derby Road station	Kings Way (via Hatfield Road, Nacton Road and Rands Way)	18 March 1928	23 April 1939; 28 June 1956 / 23 August 1963	Section from Nacton Road to Kings Way closed 23 April 1939; section from Derby Road station along Hatfield Road to Nacton Road closed 28 June 1956
6	Bishops Hill	Gainsborough Estate (Reynolds Road) (via Nacton Road and Landseer Road)	28 July 1931	23 August 1963	

Route number	From	To	Date Opened	Date Closed	Notes
3	Lattice Barn	Rushmere Heath	25 April 1934	29 April 1962	3A was short working to Lattice Barn
7	Barrack Corner (London Road)	Chantry Park	16 May 1934	29 July 1956	
	Hyde Park Corner	Electric House	16 May 1934	29 April 1962	
Unnumbered	Electric House	Colchester Road (via Woodbridge Road and Rushmere Road	6 December 1936	30 May 1959	
0	Colchester Road	Felixstowe Road (via Heath Road and Bixley Road	6 December 1936	1951	
	Electric House	Majors Corner	6 December 1936	23 August 1963	
5	Foxhall Circus	Foxhall Circus (Bixley Road)	13 December 1936	1 June 1958	
6A/6B	Gainsborough Estate (Reynolds Road)	Holbrook Road	30 January 1938	23 August 1963	Original loop at Reynolds Road removed by May 1954
7A	Hadleigh Road	Dickens Road loop	31 October 1938	July 1956	Single loop off the London Road route
2/4	Priory Heath (Nacton Road)	Felixstowe Road (via Lindbergh Road)	23 April 1939	23 August 1963	
6A/6B	Fore Street	Holbrook Road	26 February 1940	23 August 1963	Circular service; 6A anti-clockwise and 6B clockwise
6A/6B	Nacton Road	Gainsborough Estate (via Clapgate Lane)	17 December 1945	23 August 1963	Circular service; 6A anti-clockwise and 6B clockwise
11	Woodbridge Road	Sidegate Lane	10 April 1947	1 October 1959	
2A (later 2)	Nacton Road (Priory Heath)	Airport	17 August 1947	23 August 1963	
	Electric House	Cornhill (via Lloyds Avenue)	1949	July 1956	Last service X in July 1956 but wiring left in place

Evolution of routes 2 (town centre via Nacton Road to Priory Heath), 2A (town centre via St John's Road, Nacton Road and Priory Heath to Airport), 5 (town centre via St Helens Street and Grove Lane to Foxhall Road), 6/6A/6B (town centre to Gainsborough; 6A and 6B shared wiring between Electric House and the junction at Fore Street with Duke Street) and 7 (town centre via London Road to Chantry Park) and 7A (town centre via London Road to Hadleigh Road loop)

Route 2 (which became 2A)

9 June 1926	Tram service replaced by trolleybus. Service operated along St Helen's Street and along Spring Road, St John's Road and Cauldwell Hall Road to Derby Road station.
18 March 1928	Extended along Derby Road, Hatfield Road and Nacton Road, then along Rands Way and Kings Way to join existing wiring on Felixstowe Road. Returned to the town centre via Felixstowe Road, Bishops Hill as route 4, then retrace route above. Destination display Rands Circle although no turning facility at this location.
6 December 1936	Now terminated at Kings Way.
23 April 1939	Extended along Nacton Road to Lindbergh Road (Priory Heath). Return to town centre as route 4 reintroduced (see above).
1939/40	Rands Way and Kings Way wiring no longer used; retained for electrical supply purposes until 1951.
July 1947	Departure moved to Electric House; renumbered 2A
August 1947	Link with route 4 ceased; now extended along Naction Road to Airport
21 August 1949	Inward to Cornhill, then to Electric House via Westgate Street, Hyde Park Corner and Crown Street. Previously turned at the Station.
14 August 1955	Most services replaced by motorbus.
27 July 1956	Last day of trolleybus operation; replaced by motorbus.

Route 2 introduced post-1936

	Service opened to Kings Way via Bishops Hill and Nacton Road. Returned to the town centre via Felixtowe Road, Bishops Hill as route 4, the retrace the route above.
9 December 1951	Now terminated at Priory Heath; some services worked through to the airport.
23 August 1963	Last day of trolleybus operation; replaced by motorbus.

Route 5

22 December 1926	Service opened as far as Derby Road station; departure from and return to Cornhill.
29 March 1937	Further extended along Foxhall Road to a terminus adjacent to Heath Lane.
13 December 1936	Extended a short distance to join new wiring along Bixley Road and Heath Road.
By 1936	Linked cross-town with Station (route X) or Bourne Bridge (route 1).
July 1949	Departure moved to Electric House via Princes Street, Portman Road, Barrack Corner and Crown Street.
1951	Cross-town links ceased.
December 1951	Departure to Electric House now rerouted via Westgate Street, Hyde Park Corner and Crown Street.
31 May 1958	Last day of trolleybus operation; replaced by motorbus.

Routes 6/6A/6B

28 July 1931	Route 6 opened via Nacton Road and Landseer Road, terminating at Reynolds Road via 'round the houses' loop. Departure from and return to Cornhill.
6 December 1936	Departure/return moved to Electric House.

30 January 1938	Extended along Landseer Road to the junction with Holbrook Road.
26 February 1940	Extended further along Landseer Road, Holywells Road and Duke Street. Holbrook turning circle eventually removed. Now operated as two circulars: 6A outward via Hollywells Road and Landseer Road returning via Landseer Road and Nacton Road; 6B outwards via Nacton Road and Landseer Road returning via Landseer Road and Hollywells Road.
17 December 1945	Clapgate Lane wired from Nacton Road to Landseer Road; 6A and 6B now use new section in place of Nacton Road beyond Claygatte Lane.
9 December 1951	Route 6 discontinued.
23 May 1954	Reynolds Road loop removed.
23 August 1963	Last day of trolleybus operation; replaced by motorbus.

Routes 7/7A

27 March 1927	Route commenced operation along London Road to Ranelagh Road; departed from and returned to Cornhill.
16 May 1934	Extended along London Road to Chantry Park for Royal Agricultural Show.
6 December 1936	Return moved to Electric House to allow fro cross-town link services; Ranelagh Road short working became route 7A
31 October 1938	Single loop along Dickens Road and Hadleigh Road opened; this became route 7A with Ranelagh Road short working discontinued.
December 1951	Route 78 discontinued.
July 1956	Last day of route 7A trolleybus operation; replaced by motorbus.

Route number	Destination
1/1A	Bourne Bridge/Tyler Street
2/2A	Priory Heath/Airport
3/3A	Rushmere Heath/Lattice Barn
4	St Augustine's/Kings Way for depot workings
5	Foxhall Road
6A/6B	Gainsborough circulars
7/7A	Chantry Park/Hadleigh Road
8/8A	Adair Road/Bromford Road Bridge
9/9A	Whitton/Norwich Road Bidge
X	Station
11	Sidegate Lane
0/-	Colchester Road circulars

LLANELLY

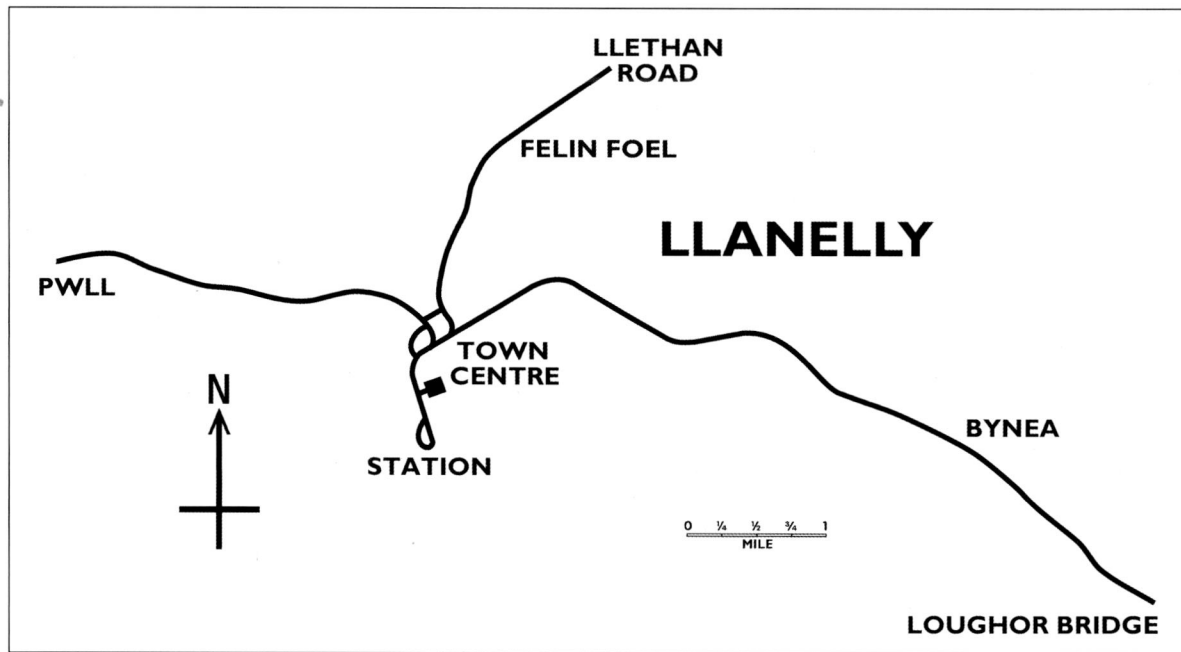

The origins of the Llanelly system lay in the Llanelly & District Lighting & Traction Co (which eventually became a subsidiary of BET), which was established in 1900 to construct an electric tramway to serve the district in place of the existing mile-long 3ft 0in gauge horse tramway that linked the town centre with the Great Western railway station.

Progress was not, however, rapid and it was not until April 1908 that the first 4ft 8½in gauge electric trams commenced operation. Alongside its tramway system, the company also owned the North Dock Power Station, which provided the power to the tramway (and later the trolleybus network).

Although the company, which changed its name to the Llanelly & District Electric Supply Co in 1924, had acquired two new double-deck trams as late as 1920, by the late 1920s the state of the local economy made modernisation of a small tramway – it only extended over 6½ route miles with a fleet of sixteen trams – uneconomic and, in November 1929, the company announced that it was seeking powers to convert the tramway to trolleybus operation. A Bill was presented to parliament two months later; this was to gain the Royal Assent on 10 July 1930 and permitted the company to convert its existing tram routes to trolleybus operation and to undertake a number of extensions. The work had to be completed within five years.

The continuing deterioration in the local economy – this was, of course, the era after the Wall Street Crash and heavy industries like coalmining and iron and steel production

The first trolleybuses delivered to the Balfour Beatty owned Llanelly & District Traction Co for the opening of the system on 17 February 1933 were fourteen Leyland TBD2s – Nos 1-12, 14 and 15 – that were fitted with Leyland-built fifty-seat bodies. One of the batch – No 5 – is seen here outside the Robinson Street depot. This was the system's only depot and had its origins in 1882 when the Llanelly Tramways Co introduced 3ft 0in gauge horse trams to the town. No 5 was one of eleven that had bodywork significantly refurbished and modified during 1948 and 1949; these vehicles also emerged in a new green and cream livery. Two were withdrawn in 1946, one in 1951 and the remainder, including No 5, during 1952. *Harry Luff/Online Transport Archive*

had suffered badly as a consequence in the Great Depression – meant that work was slow. However, the delivery of the first new trolleybuses permitted the first section – the route to Bynea (extended to Loughor Bridge) – to commence operation on 26 December 1932, having undergone the official Ministry of Transport inspection courtesy of Colonel E. P. Anderson four days earlier. The remainder of the system – the routes to Felinfoel (a short distance beyond the original tram terminus) and to Pwll – were opened on 17 February 1933, having been officially inspected four days earlier. The last trams had operated on 6 February 1933. The system as completed extended to almost 8½ route miles. The initial fleet comprised fourteen all-Leyland double-deckers; these were supplemented by seven further double-deckers delivered between 1935 and 1939.

The system as originally constructed was provided with loops at Llanelly station, the town centre and at Loughor Bridge; reversers were installed at the other termini – Felinfoel and Pwll – as well as at Pemberton and Bynea, where short workings on the Loughor Bridge route terminated. A loop was subsequently installed at Pemberton and, in 1943, at Felinfoel when a new Morris Motors Ltd vehicle factory was opened there, which required road improvements. The traffic generated by the new factory, which was inevitably engaged in the war effort at the time, resulted in the company hiring two Bournemouth trolleybuses. The final significant alteration to the system's overhead came with the opening of new Trostre strip mill and its associated housing; the decision was made to relocate the loop at Pemberton a short distance to Cefnceau; this work was undertaken over the winter of 1951/52.

The company promoted a further Bill on 27 November 1935 for a number of extensions to the network; this included a number of sections within Llanelly itself as well as western extension from Pwll to serve Burry Port and Pembrey outside the Llanelly boundary. Following local agreement to amend the proposals, the revised Act received the Royal Assent on 14 July 1936. However, no progress was made with work on the construction, with South Wales Transport countering the plan for the extension beyond Pwll by improving local bus services over the route. The powers were, however, renewed in 1941, 1944 and 1947 even though they were never acted upon.

The ultimate fate of the Llanelly system can, perhaps, be dated to 13 August 1947; it was on that date that the Electricity Act, which nationalised the electricity supply industry in Great Britain, received the Royal Assent. On 1 April 1948 North Dock Power Station passed into the ownership of the newly-established South Wales Electricity Board (created on 1 January 1948). Along with the power station, the new board also acquired the Llanelly trolleybus system.

In 1945, Llanelly & District acquired four Karrier Ws fitted with Roe-built Utility bodywork. The first of the quartet – No 37 – is seen here at the Llanelly station terminus awaiting departure to Felinfoel. After withdrawal when the system closed on 8 November 1952, all four were sold; Nos 39 and 40 went intact to Maidstone whilst the company removed the bodies of Nos 37 and 38 before the chassis were transferred to Bradford. Fitted with new East Lancs bodies, they became Nos 775 and 776 respectively. *Harry Luff/Online Transport Archive*

If the trolleybuses had been profitable, there might have been a future; however, the last year in which a surplus on the operation was gained was in 1946, when a profit of £1,503 was made. However, the following year a loss of £2,755 was incurred and, by the end of the 1950/51 financial year (not helped by a significant increase in the cost of electricity during 1950), the losses had rocketed to £7,716. As a result, the South Wales Electricity Board was keen to dispose of its loss-making subsidiary. A formal offer to purchase the system was made by South Wales Transport, a subsidiary of BET, in December 1951 and formally agreed by the board later that month. Following Ministry of Transport approval on 21 January 1952, the sale was concluded on 20 March 1952 with the transfer being officially recognised when the Llanelly District Traction Act received the Royal Assent on 1 August 1952.

At the time of the take-over, the general manger of South Wales Transport, W.M. Dravers, indicated that there was a possibility that motorbuses might replace trolleybuses; the possibility soon became a probability, however, as the 1952 Act permitted the conversion of the system; the new owners acted rapidly with the entire system being converted – without any ceremony (other than Bell Punch tickets being overprinted 'Last Trolleybus 8th November 1952') – on 8 November. Of the fleet, the twelve Utility-bodied Karrier Ws that had been new in 1945 all found new homes; two went to Maidstone whilst the chassis of the other ten were sold to Bradford and rebodied by East Lancs before re-entering service.

Two other Karrier Ws were also purchased in 1945; these were Nos 41 and 42, which received Utility bodywork supplied Brush. With one of the original Leyland TBD2s – Nos 10 – in the background, No 42 is recorded at the station terminus. Like Nos 37 and 40, the chassis of Nos 41 and 42 were sold to Bradford Corporation where, again rebodied, they became Nos 777 and 778 respectively. *C. Carter*

As members of the crew relax on the rear platform in front, passengers wait patiently on No 47 prior to departure from Llanelly station on 9 June 1952. No 47 was the penultimate of a batch of six Karrier Ws supplied with Park Royal bodywork during early 1946. On 1 April 1948 the South Wales Electricity Board, the newly-created nationalised body that resulted from the Electricity Act of 1947, assumed ownership of Llanelly's trolleybus system. Following ministerial consent, it was sold on 20 March 1952 to the South Wales Transport Co and the new owners quickly sought powers – via the Llanelly District Traction Act of 1952 – to convert the trolleybus routes to bus operation. All of the Llanelly system was converted on 8 November 1952. Following abandonment, the bodies of No 43-48 were scrapped and the chassis transferred to Bradford; again rebodied by East Lancs, the sextet entered service in the West Riding as Nos 779-84. *C. Carter/Online Transport Archive*

Fleet number	Registration	Chassis	Body	New	Withdrawn	Notes
1-12, 14 and 15	TH3004-17	Leyland TBD2	Leyland H50R	1932-33	1946-52	The bodies of 11 from the batch underwent refurbishment post-war by Welsh Metal Industries Ltd; the two not so treated – Nos 11 and 14 – were withdrawn in 1946.
16, 17	OG9886 and TH5166 (latter reregistered)	Guy BTX	Guy H60R	1930-31	1945	Ex-Guy demonstrators; ex-Birmingham 19 and 18; acquired 1935

Fleet number	Registration	Chassis	Body	New	Withdrawn	Notes
18	TH5167	Guy BTX	Guy H60R	1935	1945	
33-36	TH8906-8909	Guy BT	Weymann H56R	1937-1939	By 1952	
37-40	CBX530-533	Karrier W	Roe UH56R	1945	1952	39 and 40 sold to Maidstone; chassis of 37 and 38 to Bradford
41 and 42	CBX600-601	Karrier W	Brush UH56R	1945	1952	Chassis sold to Bradford
43-48	CBX909-914	Karrier W	PR UH56R	1946	1952	Chassis sold to Bradford
Wartime loans						
77	AEL405	Sunbeam MS2	PR H56D	1934	1945	Bournemouth 77; in service by December 1943 until June 1945; had previously been on loan to Newcastle
123	ALJ997	Sunbeam MS2	PR H56R	1935	1945	Bournemouth 123; in service by December 1943 until June 1945; had previously been on loan to Newcastle

Route number	From	To	Date Opened	Date Closed	Notes
1/2/3	Llanelly station	Loughor Bridge	26 December 1932	8 November 1952	2 short working to Bynea; 3 short working to Pemberton
6 (renumbered 3 1952)	Llanelly	Pwll	17 February 1933	8 November 1952	
5 (renumbered 2 1952)	Felinfoel	Llanelly	17 February 1933	8 November 1952	

One of the original Leyland-bodied Leyland TBD1s – No 6 – is pictured in its rebuilt form at the Pwll terminus on 9 June 1952. This was one of the batch that survived through until the final closure of the system in November 1952. *C. Carter/Online Transport Archive*

84 • BRITISH TROLLEYBUS SYSTEMS – WALES, MIDLANDS AND EAST ANGLIA

Despite its somewhat battered condition, No 4 – seen here outside the GPO on 9 June 1952 – survived in service until the final abandonment of the system. Note the traction column in the background retains the while bands painted as part of the wartime blackout precautions. The Art Deco Odeon cinema was opened on 18 June 1938; at the time it was recorded as being the first building in the town to be equipped with air conditioning. The cinema finally closed in 2012 but the building has been converted into a modern leisure facility, including a cinema screen. *C. Carter/Online Transport Archive*

Also recorded on 9 June 1952 at the GPO, this time with a service towards the station, is Karrier W No 38; the chassis of this vehicle was one of those sold to Bradford Corporation. Towards the end of the system's operation route numbers were not shown, as illustrated here, and No 38 also carries the final version of the livery with green-painted roof domes and a darker shade of green between them. *C. Carter/Online Transport Archive*

NOTTINGHAM

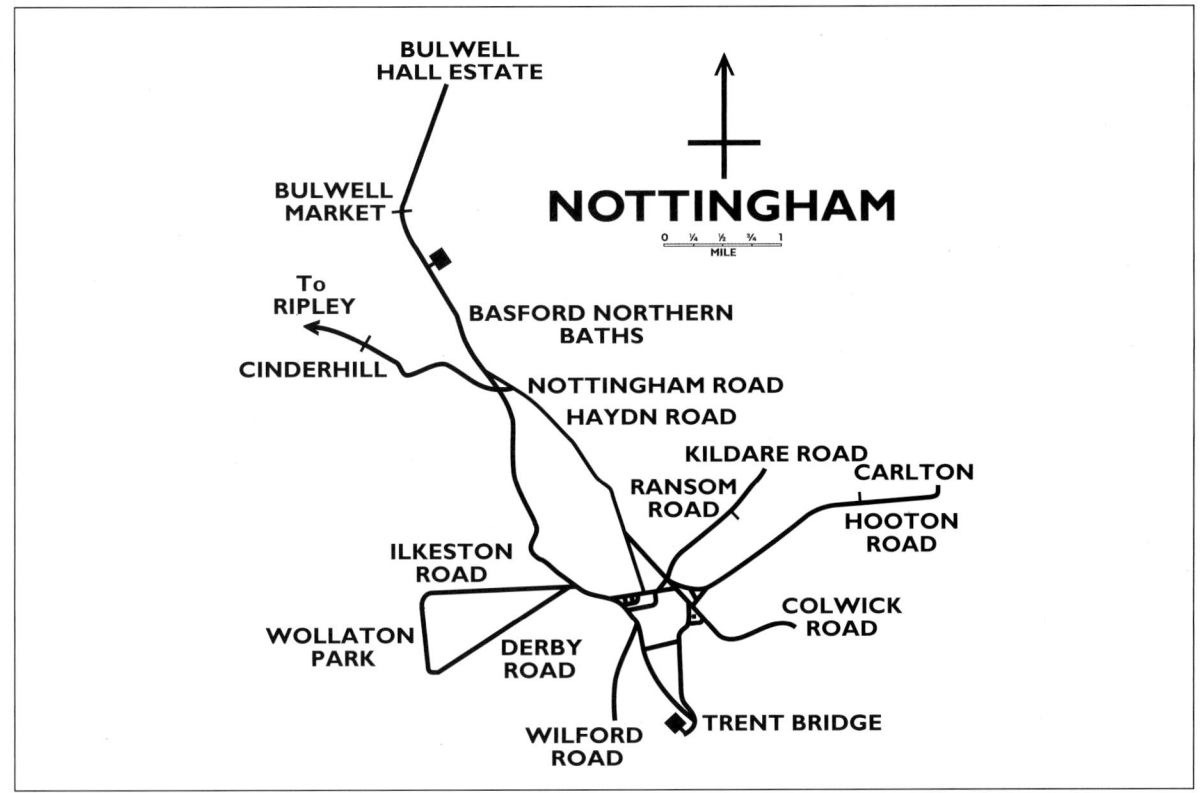

Having taken over the horse tramways operated in the city, Nottingham Corporation introduced standard gauge electric trams on 1 January 1901 and the system eventually grew to 25½ route miles, making it the largest tramway to serve the East Midlands (that operated by Leicester Corporation was slightly smaller). However, unlike Leicester where the trams were to survive until after the Second World War, those of Nottingham were to disappear by the mid-1930s.

On 15 August 1913, Royal Assent was given to the Nottingham Corporation Act 1913; amongst powers granted in the Act, alongside a number of tramway extensions, was the right to operate trolleybuses between Market Place and Trent Bridge – the Bill's original plans for a service through to West Bridgford had been dropped following opposition from West Bridgford UDC – as well as for the use of trolleybuses over any tram route. However, there was no further progress on the introduction of trolleybuses at this time.

After the First World War, the future of the Nottingham Road via Sherwood Rise and Ingham Road route came under consideration; although much of the Nottingham tramway network was double track by the date, this route still included sections of single track with passing loops (as did the outer sections of a number of other routes such as

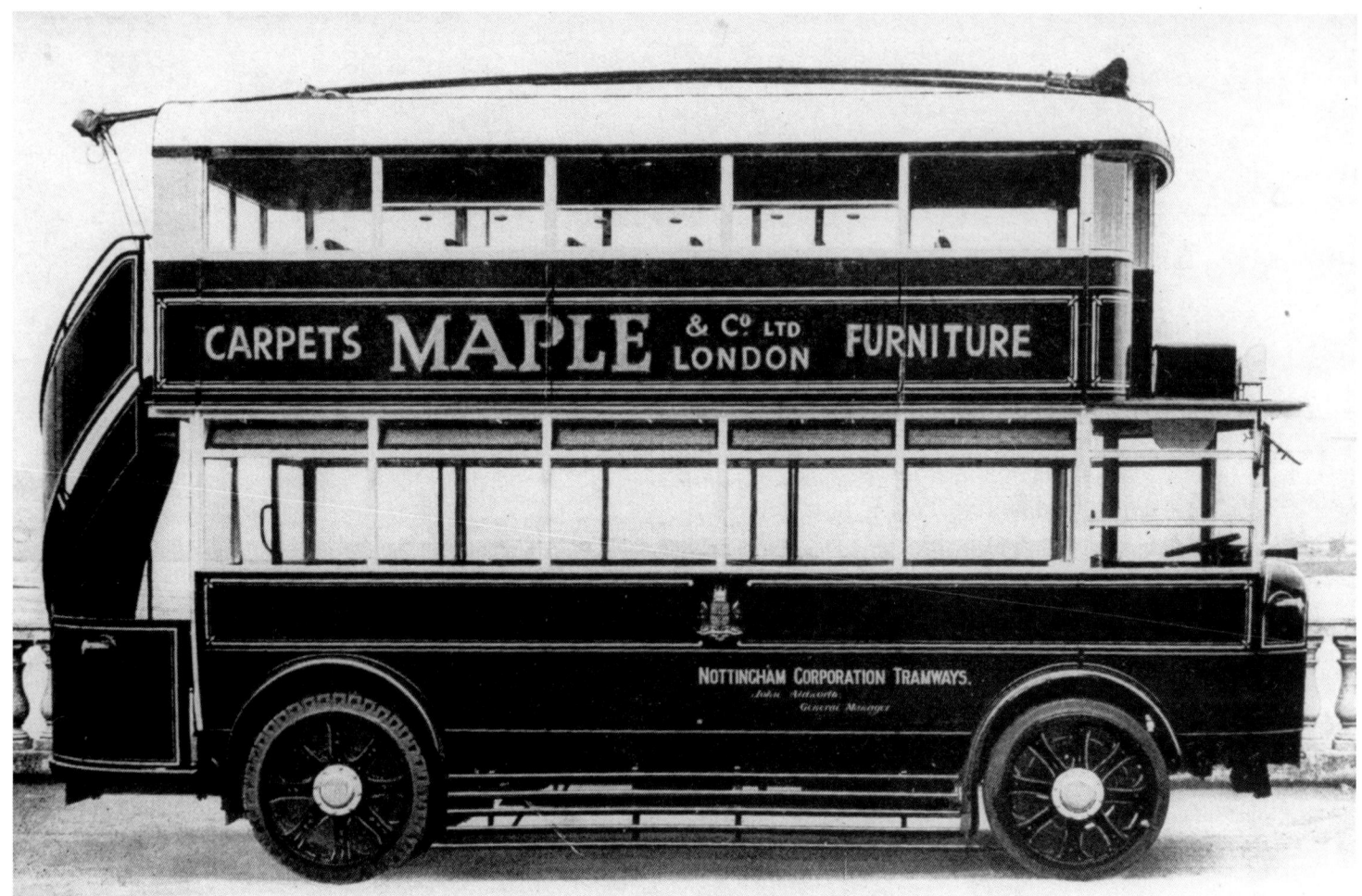

For the opening of the Nottingham system on 10 April 1927 Railless supplied ten chassis, production of which had been subcontracted to Short Brothers, that were fitted with fifty-two-seat open-staircase double-deck bodies also manufactured by Short as evinced by this side view of one of the batch. No 10, which differed slightly from No 1-9, had been used previously as a demonstrator by Railless. All were withdrawn between 1932 and 1935. *Barry Cross Collection/Online Transport Archive*

those to Arnold and Carlton). Following a visit to the recently converted Nechells route in Birmingham in January 1924, it was decided to obtain powers to convert the Nottingham Road route; these were confirmed by the Nottingham Corporation Act 1925, which received the Royal Assent on 7 August 1925. This covered the Nottingham Road route as well as the tram routes to Wells Road and Wilford Road.

For the new service, Nottingham ordered ten double-deckers; although supplied by Railless Ltd, the ten were designed and built by Short Bros and were the last vehicles supplied through Railless Ltd. Thereafter Short Bros ceased to produce trolleybuses chassis, concentrating on other – more profitable – work. The new route – from a loop in the city centre using King Street, Queen Street and Upper Parliament Street – through to a terminus adjacent to the Bulwell tram route on Ingham road opened on 10 April 1927. The arrival of the trolleybuses also heralded a new livery: green replaced the maroon used on the trams. The success of the new service meant that additional vehicles were required; with Railless Ltd no longer in the market, two double-deckers were acquired from Ransomes, Sims & Jefferies.

For the conversion of the routes to Wells Road – which involved a short extension beyond the existing tram terminus – and Wilford Road, a further twelve trolleybuses

The Ipswich-based Ransomes, Sims & Jefferies had delivered two additional vehicles – Nos 11 and 12 – to supplement the existing fleet and, with the planned opening of the route from Wells Road to Wilford Road a further twelve trolleybuses were ordered. The order was split, with Ransomes, Sims & Jefferies supplying Nos 13-18. These were based around the manufacturer's D6 chassis and Ransomes also constructed the sixty-seat bodywork. Renumbered 313-18 in 1939, this wartime view of No 315 – note the censored fleetname and the white painted mudguards (to aid visibility during the blackout) – records the vehicle on a service to Carlton. *D.W.K. Jones Collection/Online Transport Archive*

were ordered in 1929; following their delivery, the Wilford Road to Wells Road route commenced operation on 23 February 1930. With the two routes comprising about 5½ route miles the corporation developed ambitious plans for the expansion of the system, although opposition from Trent Motor Traction and Nottinghamshire County Council resulted in a more restricted vision once the Nottingham Corporation Act 1930 received the Royal Assent on 10 July 1930. This Act permitted the conversion of the remaining tram routes and extensions within the corporation's boundaries.

The first section to be converted after the 1930 Act was that to Wollaton Park; this was served by two routes: that via Derby Road was previously served by tram whilst that via Ilkeston Road was by motorbus. Both were replaced by a new circular service that commenced operation on 29 November 1931. The Wollaton Park service was linked to that to Carlton following the conversion of the tram route to the latter on 20 March 1932. The Carlton tram route extended beyond the borough boundary – and was comprised largely of single track with passing loops beyond that point – and the new trolleybus route extended beyond the original tram terminus to Post Office Square.

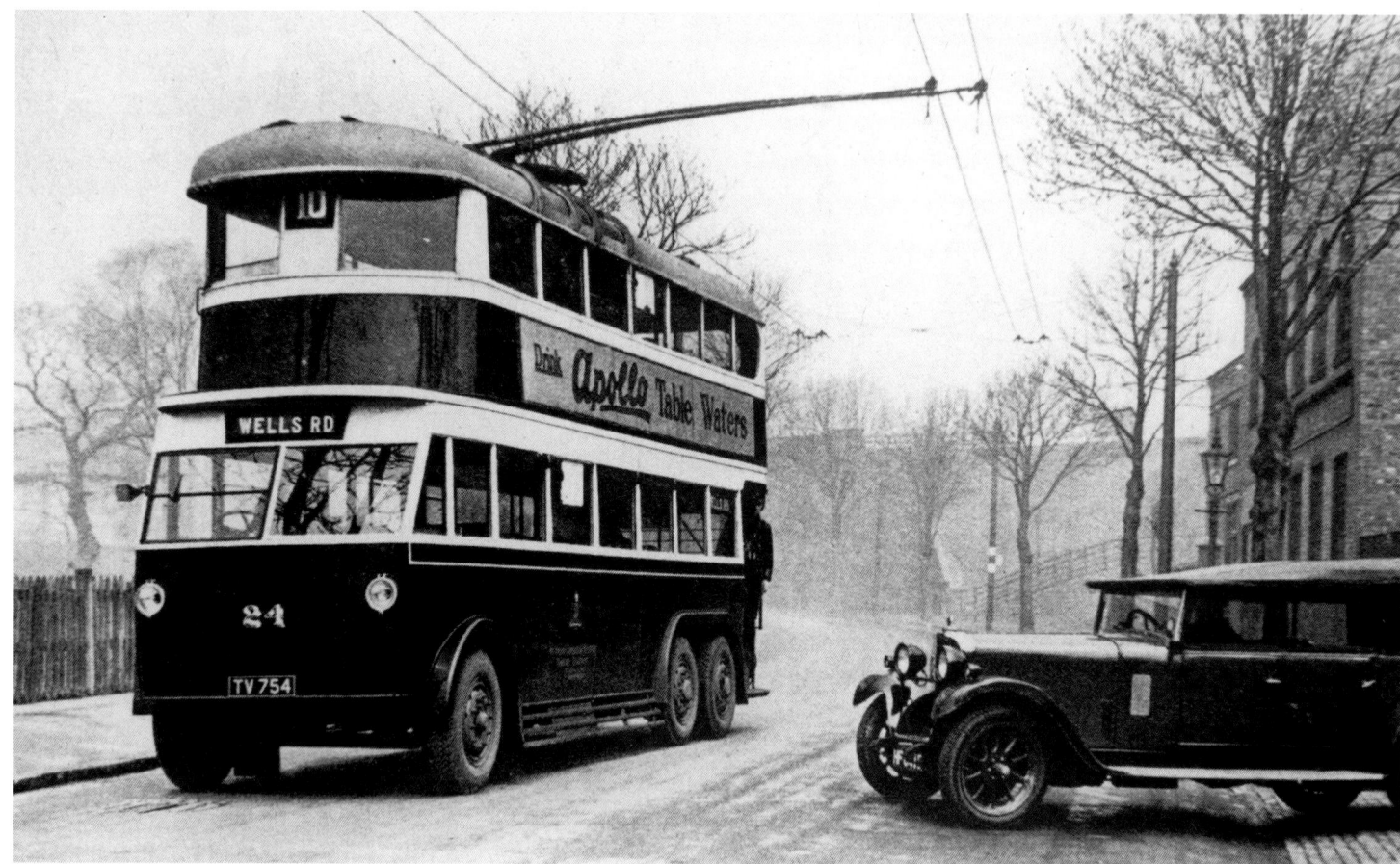

In 1930 Nottingham took delivery of a batch of six English Electric E11s fitted with the same supplier's sixty-seat bodywork. The batch, along with the Ransomes, Sims & Jefferies-built Nos 13-18, was delivered for the opening of the Wells Road to Wilford Road service and here the last of the batch, No 24, is seen posed to demonstrate the flexibility of the trolleybuses. No 24 was decorated in 1937 to mark the coronation of George VI. All six, which had been renumbered 319-24 in 1939, were withdrawn between 1944 and 1948. *Barry Cross Collection/Online Transport Archive*

The next extension, from the original Nottingham Road terminus was the route to Cinderhill; this connected into the extension of the Notts & Derby route and the company commenced through operation over the route into central Nottingham on 5 October 1933; it was not until 10 October 1933 that the corporation introduced a part day service to Cinderhill.

The next route to be converted was the long north-south service from Trent Bridge to Bulwell Market; this commenced operation, along with a northern extension to Bulwell Hall Estate, on 13 May 1934. The final extensions to the system occurred on 2 June 1935 when trolleybuses were introduced to the section from the city centre to Trent Bridge via London Road and to the Colwick Road route.

Although there remained two tramway services operational – the long routes north-eastwards to Arnold and Mapperley – these were destined to be replaced by motorbus with the last trams operating on 5 September 1936. One factor in the changed policy was the appointment of a new general manager – J.L. Gunn from Aberdeen – who was not a believer in trolleybuses; he commented 'When the trolleybus programme was drawn up, the heavy-oil [diesel] vehicle was nowhere near its present stage of perfection, and accurate comparisons were not possible.' Gunn's arrival may well have facilitated the sale of nineteen of Nottingham's most modern trams to his erstwhile employers following their withdrawal.

Following an accident to No 8 which led to its withdrawal, a single Karrier chassis was purchased in 1933. This was fitted with the Brush sixty-seat body that had originally been fitted to the Thornycroft demonstrator operated during 1930 and 1931. The resulting vehicle is pictured here during the Second World War. It was withdrawn in 1948. *Barry Cross Collection/Online Transport Archive*

There were proposals in 1938 and again in 1939 for the conversion of the system to motorbus operation but nothing was undertaken and the increased traffic during the war resulted in the expansion of the fleet through the arrival of second-hand vehicles from Cleethorpes Corporation, Southend-on-Sea Corporation and Hastings & District as well as five 8ft 0in wide vehicles that had been originally destined for export to South Africa. Later in the war these were supplemented by a number of Utility-bodied Karrier Ws. The wartime years also saw proposals for the extension of the system; however, despite the fact that these would have relieved use of scarce diesel, none were progressed.

Between 1946 and 1952 the corporation took delivery of 129 new two- and three-axle trolleybuses. These deliveries permitted the withdrawal of all of the surviving pre-war trolleybuses as well as those that had been acquired second-hand. Although the bodywork for the final two batches had initially been contracted to Metro-Cammell, delays meant that the work was transferred to Roe. The first contraction occurred on 25 April 1953 when Notts & Derby converted its system to motorbus operation; this was, however, countered by the corporation converting its part-day service to Cinderhill into a new all-day service that connected through to Trent Bridge from the following day.

The system operated largely unchanged for a decade. However, in 1961 a decision was taken to convert the trolleybus services to motorbus operation. The appointment of John C. Wake as general manager in July 1962 meant that the programme of conversion was accelerated. As general manager previously at St Helens (1952-61) and Bradford (1961/62) he had demonstrated a desire to eliminate trolleybuses and he was quick to adopt a similar policy in Nottingham.

The first phase of the programme commenced on 2 November 1962 with the conversion of the section from Trent Bridge to Wollaton via London Road and Derby Road. This was followed – prompted by redevelopment within the city centre – on 1 April 1965 by the conversion of the route from Trent Bridge to Bulwell Market; this resulted in the closure to trolleybus services of Trent Bridge depot (the surviving routes were all served by the depots at Bulwell, until 31 May 1965, and Parliament Street [previously known as Carter Gate] until final conversion). The overhead from the city centre to Bulwell Market remained in use until 1 June 1965 when the service from Bulwell Hall Estate to Colwick Road was converted. The Cinderhill route was converted on 1May 1965. On 30 September 1965 the route from Carlton to Wollaton was converted; the short working from the city centre to Hooton remained operational until the end of the year. On 9 October 1965 it was the turn of the Wells Road to Wilford Road service to be converted.

The final conversion of the tram system during 1935 and 1936 saw a substantial increase in the size of the trolleybus fleet, with fifty-six new double-deckers entering service in 1934. Of these, thirty-five were Karrier E6s fitted with either Metro-Cammell sixty-four-seat bodywork (Nos 51-60) or equivalent bodywork by Brush (Nos 61-85). Another wartime view records No 57 – by this date renumbered 357 – with additions for use during the war; more evident in this view is the shields fitted over the headlights, although fitted with a fog light, a further precaution for use during the blackout. All of the Karrier E6s were withdrawn between 1948 and 1950; although not preserved at the time, one of the Brush-bodied examples – No 367 – was subsequently rescued and is under restoration at Sandtoft.
John Meredith Collection/Online Transport Archive

These conversions left one main route operational; this was the original service from the city centre to Nottingham Road. This with its short working to Haydn Road soldiered on for a further eight months; the last public services were operated on 30 June 1966. The following day an official farewell – using an appropriately decorated No 506 – was operated. Of the Nottingham fleet, five of the post-war deliveries – including No 506 – survive as does one of the pre-war Karrier E6s with English Electric bodywork – No 367 – which was rescued more than ten years after withdrawal in 1962. The chassis of a seventh vehicle – No 46 (one of the Ransomes, Sims & Jefferies double-deckers of 1932) – was acquired in 1999 almost 50 years after the complete vehicle was acquired as a store following withdrawal in 1950.

On 23 April 1950, Leyland TTB3 No 436 is pictured at the Bulwell Hall Estate terminus. This was the last of a batch of thirty – original number 107-36 – that were fitted with Metro-Cammell sixty-four-seat bodywork. These were the only Leyland-badged trolleybuses operated by Nottingham and were also unusual in having a large destination box at the front. The first two were withdrawn in 1949 and all had been taken out of service by the end of 1952. The Bulwell Hall Estate service – route 44 – was converted to bus operation on 1 June 1965. *John Meredith/Online Transport Archive*

Above: **Between 1943** and 1945 Nottingham was allocated twenty-one wartime Karrier Ws fitted with Utility fifty-six-seat bodywork from a number of manufacturers. The first four – Nos 442-45 – had bodywork supplied by Weymann as did Nos 455-58; Park Royal bodywork was fitted to Nos 452-54 whilst Nos 459-65 and Nos 466-68 were bodied by Roe and Brush respectively. Here the first of the type – No 442 – is seen on King Street/Queen Street on 21 August 1951. Unlike a number of other operators, Nottingham did not rebody its Utility vehicles after the war and withdrawals commenced in 1957 with the last two being withdrawn in 1965; No 466 is preserved. *C. Carter/Online Transport Archive*

Right: **One of** the Roe-bodied Utility Karrier Ws – No 460 – is pictured at the terminus at Wilford Bridge; this route was converted to bus operation on 9 October 1965. *Harry Luff/Online Transport Archive*

Above: **After the** war, Nottingham acquired two further batches of Karrier Ws. The first were Nos 469-78 that were new in 1946; although post-war deliveries, the fifty-six-seat bodywork supplied by Park Royal was largely unchanged from the Utility bodywork on Nos 452-54 as evinced by the first of the batch – No 469 – seen on Market Place on 23 July 1962. By this date, the last of the type were approaching withdrawal; all were taken out of service between 1959 and 1965. *Gerald Druce/Online Transport Archive*

Left: **Pictured at** Cinderhill during a Southern Counties Touring Society tour of the system on 19 July 1959 is BUT 9611T No 487. This was one of thirteen vehicles – Nos 483-95 – that were new in 1948. Fitted with Roe fifty-six-seat bodywork – the last trolleybuses delivered to Nottingham by this supplier – the batch represented the last two-axle trolleybuses purchased by the corporation. No 493 was exhibited at the 1948 Commercial Motor Show and was eventually to be preserved. All were withdrawn between 1963 and 1965. *John Meredith/Online Transport Archive*

Above: The second batch of post-war Karrier Ws – Nos 479-82 – were a quartet of Roe-bodied examples that were delivered in 1948. Here the last of the four is pictured on Lister Gate heading towards Trent Bridge with a service on route 48 on 20 August 1951. All four were finally withdrawn in 1965. *C. Carter/Online Transport Archive*

Right: Nottingham's final trolleybus deliveries came in the form of two batches of three-axle BUT 9641Ts bodied by Brush. The first twenty-five – Nos 500-24 – were delivered during 1949 and 1950 and here No 518 is pictured at the Carlton terminus of route 39. No 506 was selected to become Nottingham's final trolleybus; it and No 502 were both preserved following withdrawal. *Harry Luff/Online Transport Archive*

Pictured overtaking 1956 vintage AEC Regent V No 223 on Long Row is No 581; this was one of seventy-seven BUT 9641Ts fitted with 7ft 6in seventy-seat bodywork supplied by Brush. New during 1951 and 1952, these were the last new trolleybuses received by the corporation and permitted the withdrawal of the last of the pre-war vehicles. No 565 – in the guise of No 563 – was exhibited at the 1950 Commercial Motor Show. The service to Wells Road was converted to bus operation on 9 October 1965. All of this batch of BUTs was withdrawn during 1965 and 1966 with No 578 being preserved. *Marcus Eavis/Online Transport Archive*

Fleet number	Registration	Chassis	Body	New	Withdrawn	Notes
1-10	TO5002-5011	Railless LF (built by Short Bros)	Short H52ROS	1927 (1925 in the case of 10)	1932-35	10 had been a Railless demonstrator and had been exhibited at the 1925 Industrial Commercial Motor Exhibition
11-12	TO8621-8622	RS&J D4	RS&J H52R	1929	1936	
13-18 (renumbered 313-18 in 1939)	TV743-748	RS&J D6	RS&J H60R	1930	1945-46	
19-24 (renumbered 319-24 in 1939)	TV749-754	EE E11	EE H56R	1930	1944-48	
25		AEC		1930		Demonstrator; returned to supplier
26		Guy		1930		Demonstrator; returned to supplier
27 (renumbered 50 when acquired and to 350 in 1939)	VH3305	Karrier-Clough	PR H60R	1930 (on loan initially)	1948	Demonstrator; acquired 1932

Fleet number	Registration	Chassis	Body	New	Withdrawn	Notes
28		Thorneycroft	Brush H60R	1930	1931	Demonstrator; chassis returned to supplier; body transferred to new 1 1933
25-36 (renumbered 325-36 in 1939)	TV4463-4474	Karrier-Clough E6	PR H60R	1931-32	1948-50	
37-49 (renumbered 337-49 in 1939)	TV4475-4487	RS&J D6	Brush H60R	1931-32	1948-50	Chassis of 46 preserved at Sandtoft
1 (renumbered 301 in 1939)	TV8473	Karrier E6	Brush H60R	1933	1948	Acquired to replace 8 after an accident; body reused from 28
51-60 (renumbered 351-60 in 1939)	TV9313/9315/9316/9310/9311/9312/9317/9314/9308/9309	Karrier E6	Metro-Cammell H64R	1934	By 1952	
61-85 (renumbered 361-85 in 1939)	TV9327/9328/9319/9320/9331-9334/9336/9340/9317/9318/9829/9830/9321-9326/9337/9338/9335/9341/9342	Karrier E6	Brush H64R	1934	1950-52	367 preserved
86-106 (renumbered 386-406 in 1939)	TV9343-9347/9353/9354/9350/9351/9355/9363/9357/9362/9356/9358/9348/9359/9361/9352/9360	RS&J D6	Brush H64R	1934	1948-51	
107-36 (renumbered 407-36 in 1939)	ATV170-199	Leyland TTB3	MCW H64R	1935	1949-52	
437-40	FW8995, AFU153-155	AEC 661T	PR H56R	1937-38	1952	Ex-Cleethorpes 59-62; acquired 1940
302 and 303	JN60-61	EE	EE H56R	1930	1945	Ex-Southend 110 and 111; acquired 1940.
441	GTO741	Daimler CTM4	Weymann H54R	1938	1952	Ex-demonstrator; acquired 1941
304-09	DY5111/5120/5121/5126, 5483, 5578	Guy BTX	RS&J B32C	1928-30	1946	Ex-Hastings 9, 18, 19, 24, 40 and 51; acquired 1941

Fleet number	Registration	Chassis	Body	New	Withdrawn	Notes
442-45	GTV42-45	Karrier W	Weymann UH56R	1943-44	1960-62	
447-51	GTV47-51	Sunbeam MF2	Weymann UH56R	1942	1957-58	Originally ordered by Johannesburg but diverted due to the war
452-54	GTV652-654	Karrier W	PR UH56R	1944	1957-62	
455-58	GTV655-658	Karrier W	Weymann UH56R	1944	1960	
459-65	GTV659-665	Karrier W	Roe UH56R	1945	1962-65	
466-68	GTV666-668	Karrier W	Brush UH56R	1945	1962-65	466 preserved
469-78	HAU169-178	Karrier W	PR H56R	1946	1959-65	
479-82	KTV479-482	Karrier W	Roe H56R	1948	1965	
483-95	KTV483-495	BUT 9611T	Roe H56R	1948	1963-65	493 preserved
500-24	KTV500-524	BUT 9641T	Brush H60R	1949-50	1963-66	8ft wide bodywork; 502 and 506 preserved
525-601	KTV525-601	BUT 9641T	Brush H60R	1951-52	1965-66	578 preserved

Route number	From	To	Date Opened	Date Closed	Notes
5 later 36	King Street / Queen Street	Nottingham Road	10 April 1927	30 June 1966	H later 37 was short working to Haydn Road
10 later 40	Wilford Road	St Anne's Well Road (Kildare Road)	23 February 1930	9 October 1965	47 was short working to Ransom Road from Wilford Bridge
8 and 9 later 38, 39 and 45	City Centre	Wollaton Park (via Derby Road and via Ilkeston Road)	29 November 1931	3 November 1962 (route 45 via London Road and Derby Road); 30 September 1965 (route 39 via Ilkeston Road)	Circular service; later linked with service to Carlton (38 until 9 January 1937 and 39) and to Trent Bridge (45)
8 and 9 later 38 and 39	City Centre	Carlton	20 March 1932	30 September 1965 / End 1965	38 operated via Derby Road until 9 January 1937; 39 was via Ilkeston Road; 38 was subsequently peak hour service to Hooton Road from 6 April 1941; services continued to use the section to the short working reverser at Hooton until the end of 1965

Route number	From	To	Date Opened	Date Closed	Notes
41	Cinderhill	Queen Street via Nottingham Road	5 October 1933 (corporation service introduced 10 October 1933)	1 May 1965	Also used by trolleybuses from Notts & Derby on route A1 until 25 April 1953; 41 operated through to Trent Bridge after 26 April 1953 in place of service 48
43	Trent Bridge	Bulwell Market	13 May 1934	1 April 1965 (route 43); section from Bulwell Market to City Centre used by route 45 until 1 June 1965	Via Arkwright Street; 42 was peak hours short working to Basford Northern Baths; 48 was Trent Bridge to Nottingham Road service until 25 April 1953
44	Bulwell Market	Bulwell Hall Estate	13 May 1934	1 June 1965	
44	City Centre	Colwick Road	2 June 1935	1 June 1965	
45	City Centre	Trent Bridge	2 June 1935	3 November 1962	Via London Road

Service numbers	Route
5 (later 36)	King Street/Queen Street to Nottingham Road
H (later 37)	King Street/Queen Street to Haydn Road (short working of route 5/36)
8 (later 38)	Carlton to Wollaton Park via Derby Road (until 9 January 1937; replaced by route 45)
38	Hooton Road to King Street/Queen Street later Theatre Square (from 6 April 1941)
9 (later 39)	Carlton to Wollaton Park via Ilkeston Road
10 (later 40)	Kildare Road (Wells Road) to Wilford Road
41	King Street/Queen Street to Cinderhill (until 25 April 1953)
41	Trent Bridge to Cinderhill (from 26 April 1953 in place of route 48)
42	Basford Northern Baths to Old Market Square
43	Trent Bridge to Bulwell Market
44	Bulwell Hall Estate to Colwick Road
45	Trent Bridge to Wollaton Park via Derby Road (from 10 January 1937; replaced route 38)
46	Old Market Square to Trent Bridge
47	Ransom Road (Wells Road) to Wilford Road (short working of route 40)
48	Trent Bridge to Nottingham Road (until 25 April 1953; replaced by new route 41)

NOTTS & DERBY

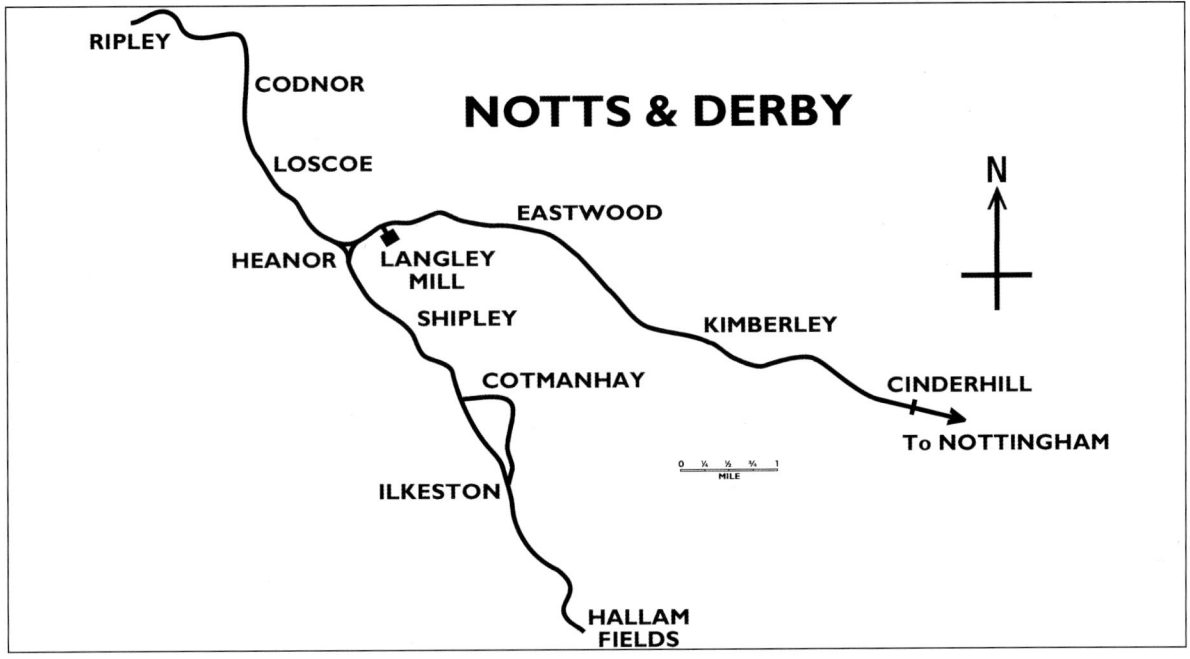

At the start of the twentieth century there were proposals that would have resulted in a network of more than ninety route miles of tramway linking Derby, Mansfield and Nottingham. Unsurprisingly, the local railway companies – the Great Central, Great Northern and Midland – took objection to this potential new competitor and, in the event, only one section was to be constructed – that from Cinderhill, where a connection was made to the standard gauge tramways planned and built by Nottingham Corporation (the corporation route was also originally part of the larger scheme; only company trams operated over the corporation-built section from Cinderhill to Vernon Road) to Ripley – a distance of almost 11½ route miles.

The Nottinghamshire & Derbyshire Tramways Co – generally abbreviated to Notts & Derby – struggled to raise the funds for the enterprise but eventually its share capital was provided by the Tramways, Light & Power Co (later the Midland Counties Electricity Supply Co), which itself was a subsidiary of Balfour Beatty.

The company's route finally opened in stages during July and August 1913 with through services operating to central Nottingham commencing on 1 January 1914. This was not quite the final stage in the company's development of tramways as it took over operation of the 3¾ route mile 3ft 6in gauge tramway operated by Ilkeston UDC on 16 November 1916; the company purchased the tramway outright in 1922.

Like a number of other tramways, Notts & Derby suffered from unfettered bus competition after the First World War and, with a route largely formed of single track

The first trolleybuses acquired by the Nottinghamshire & Derbyshire Traction Co – or Notts & Derby as it was better known – were six English Electric single-deckers – Nos 300-05 – that were equipped with the same manufacturers thirty-two-seat bodywork; No 301 is pictured here when virtually brand new. Delivered for the opening of the system on 7 January 1932, the six were destined for a relatively short career with the company, being sold to Mexborough & Swinton in 1937. *John Meredith Collection/Online Transport Archive*

with passing loops, was particularly vulnerable. The associated Midland General Omnibus Co – incorporated on 19 June 1920 and another Balfour Beatty subsidiary – commenced operation in 1922.

Despite opposition – the MP for Ilkeston, George Oliver, spoke for some length in the House of Commons on 3 July 1928 against the Bill, for example – the Nottinghamshire & Derbyshire Tramways (Trolley Vehicles, etc) Bill was passed; this authorised, inter alia, the company to convert its tramway services to trolleybus operation as well as allowing for their extension between Ilkeston and Heanor to connect the two systems. The company's official name changed to the Nottinghamshire & Derbyshire Traction Co subsequent to the powers being granted.

On 6 February 1931, trams were withdrawn from the sole Ilkeston route from Cotmanhay to Hallam Fields with buses temporarily taking over whilst the route was converted to trolleybus operation. For the opening of the Cotmanhay to Hallam Fields section on 7 January 1932, English Electric supplied six single-deckers; these were destined not to remain with Notts & Derby for long, being sold to Mexborough & Swinton in 1937.

The next section to open was that from Cotmanhay to Ripley via Heanor allied to the Cotmanhay bypass; the route to Heanor was that not previously operated by tram.

In 1933, Notts & Derby took delivery of its first double-deckers; Nos 317-31 were AEC 661Ts fitted with Metro-Cammell fifty-five-seat bodywork and were acquired for the opening of the section from Heanor to Cinderhill on 5 October 1933 and the start of through running over the Nottingham Corporation system into the centre of the city. Pictured here is No 328 heading inbound at Cinderhill with a service towards King Street/Queen Street. All of the batch were withdrawn in 1949 following the delivery of the fifteen BUT 9611Ts, Nos 343-57. Note the turn back into Notts & Derby territory towards Kimberley. *Barry Cross Collection/Online Transport Archive*

With the delivery of a further ten single-deckers, this time supplied by AEC, services from Heanor to Cotmanhay commenced on 1 August 1932. Apart from loops at Hallam Fields, Park Road (where the company's ex-Ilkeston depot was situated), Cotmanhay and Ilkeston, there was also a short working at Shipley where a trolley reverser was installed.

The final phase in the development of the Notts & Derby system covered the route from Heanor to Nottingham via Cinderhill. Through tram services beyond Cinderhill into Nottingham ended in 1932 with Nottingham Corporation undertaking the conversion of the overhead on the Cinderhill route. Notts & Derby trams continued to operate between Cinderhill and Heanor; regular services had ceased on 30 December 1932, but peak hour services and the operation of at least one tram through the day, for legal reasons, continued until 4 October 1933 whilst the trolleybus overhead was erected.

With work completed, trolleybus services commenced on the section from Heanor to Nottingham on 5 October 1933; until the cessation of company trolleybus operations in 1953, that from Vernon Road to Cinderhill was mainly operated by the company – all day corporation services to Cinderhill only commenced in late April 1953. For the new services, a batch of fifteen AEC 661Ts fitted with Metro-Cammell bodywork were delivered. This opening meant that the Notts & Derby system was now complete. A further seven AEC 661Ts, this time bodied by Weymann (a company that was to body all of the company's subsequent trolleybuses), were delivered in 1937; these replaced the batch of single-deckers withdrawn and sold to Mexborough & Swinton. A further ten vehicles were ordered but these were delayed and not received until 1941 and 1942. The last vehicles to be acquired were fifteen BUT 9611Ts in 1949; these vehicles allowed for the withdrawal of the surviving pre-war trolleybuses.

Although there were proposals, both pre- and post-war, to extend the system, most notably a second link with the corporation system through a route linking Ilkeston with Wollaton, none of these progressed. Despite the purchase of the new trolleybuses in 1949, Notts & Derby saw its future as a bus operator. As elsewhere, the nationalisation in 1948 of the company's power station meant that the trolleybuses were no longer supporting a group company and were forced to pay the market price for power. Given that Notts & Derby was a subsidiary of the Midland Counties Electricity Supply Co, nationalisation also meant that the trolleybuses passed into state control, initially to the British Electricity Authority and then in 1949, to the British Transport Commission.

On 1 August 1952, Royal Assent was given to the Nottinghamshire & Derbyshire Traction Act of 1952. This empowered the company to convert its trolleybus services to bus and, on 25 April 1953, trolleybuses were withdrawn from the entire system. Although the Notts & Derby system had closed, this was not to be the end for the fleet; Bradford Corporation acquired all thirty-two remaining trolleybuses. All re-entered service retaining their original bodywork initially, the ten wartime AECs, however, were all subsequently rebodied by East Lancs.

Whilst no Notts & Derby trolleybuses were secured for preservation at closure, two of the post-war BUTs – Nos 353 and 357 – were saved following their withdrawal in the West Riding during the summer of 1967. More recently, one of the AEC 662Ts of 1932, which was withdrawn in 1949, has also been rescued for restoration.

AEC 661T No 334 stands at the Hallam Fields terminus prior to heading towards Ilkeston and Cotmanhay. No 334 was one of a batch of five vehicles delivered during 1941 that were fitted with Weymann fifty-six-seat bodywork. The vehicles were designed to cope with additional traffic as a result of the war. Following the conversion of the system to bus operation in April 1953 all five were sold to Bradford Corporation where, retaining their original bodies, they re-entered service as No 587-91 during 1953 and 1954 before being withdrawn for rebodying later in the decade. *Marcus Eavis /Online Transport Archive*

Above: **The last** new trolleybuses purchased by Notts & Derby were fifteen BUT 9611Ts – Nos 343-57 – that were delivered in 1949. These were fitted with Weymann fifty-six-seat bodywork and were to survive until the system's conversion on 25 April 1953. Barely four years old when withdrawn, all fifteen were acquired by Bradford Corporation, where they re-entered service as Nos 760-74. Withdrawn in Bradford as a result of the conversion of the Wakefield Road routes in 1967, two of the batch – Nos 353 (seen here awaiting departure from central Nottingham on 21 August 1951) and 357 – were subsequently preserved. *C. Carter/Online Transport Archive*

Left: **Notts &** Derby acquired a further batch of five AEC 661Ts fitted with Weymann bodywork in 1942; like the earlier batch, No 338-42 were sold to Bradford Corporation in 1953 where they became Nos 582-96. The five were also rebuilt by East Lancs in 1958, eventually being withdrawn in the West Riding between 1965 and 1968. Here No 341 – later Bradford No 595 – is seen in Heanor prior to forming a service on route A2 to Hallam Fields. *Harry Luff/Online Transport Archive*

Fleet number	Registration	Chassis	Body	New	Withdrawn	Notes
300-05	RB5568-5573	EE	EE B32F	1932	1937	Sold to Mexborough & Swinton
306-15	RB6613-6622	AEC 662T	EE B32F	1932	1949	307 preserved
316	UK9601	Guy BT32	Guy B32F	1930	1949	Guy demonstrator; acquired 1932
317-31	RB8951-8965	AEC 661T	MCCW H55R	1933	1949	
300-05/32	DRB616-622	AEC 661T	Weymann H56R	1937	1953	Sold to Bradford
333-37	HNU826-830	AEC 661T	Weymann H56R	1941	1953	Sold to Bradford
338-42	HNU970-974	AEC 661T	Weymann H56R	1942	1953	Sold to Bradford
343-57	HNU224-38	BUT 9611T	Weymann H56R	1949	1953	Sold to Bradford; 353 and 357 preserved

Route number	From	To	Date Opened	Date Closed	Notes
A2 (A3 bypassing Cotmanhay)	Cotmanhay	Hallam Fields	7 January 1932	25 April 1953	A3 terminated at Rutland Hotel in Ilkeston
A2 (A3 bypassing Cotmanhay)	Cotmanhay (including Cotmanhay bypass)	Heanor	1 August 1932	25 April 1953	
A1	Heanor	Ripley	1 August 1932	25 April 1953	
A1	Heanor	Cinderhill (for through services to Nottingham)	5 October 1933	25 April 1953	

With the church of St Bartholomew's, Hallam Fields, as the backdrop, No 343 is seen awaiting departure with a service on route 2A to Cotmanhay. At the time of writing, the late Victorian church with its Grade II listed tower is now redundant; the building, looking increasingly in poor condition, is currently to let. *J. H. Roberts/Online Transport Archyive*

PONTYPRIDD

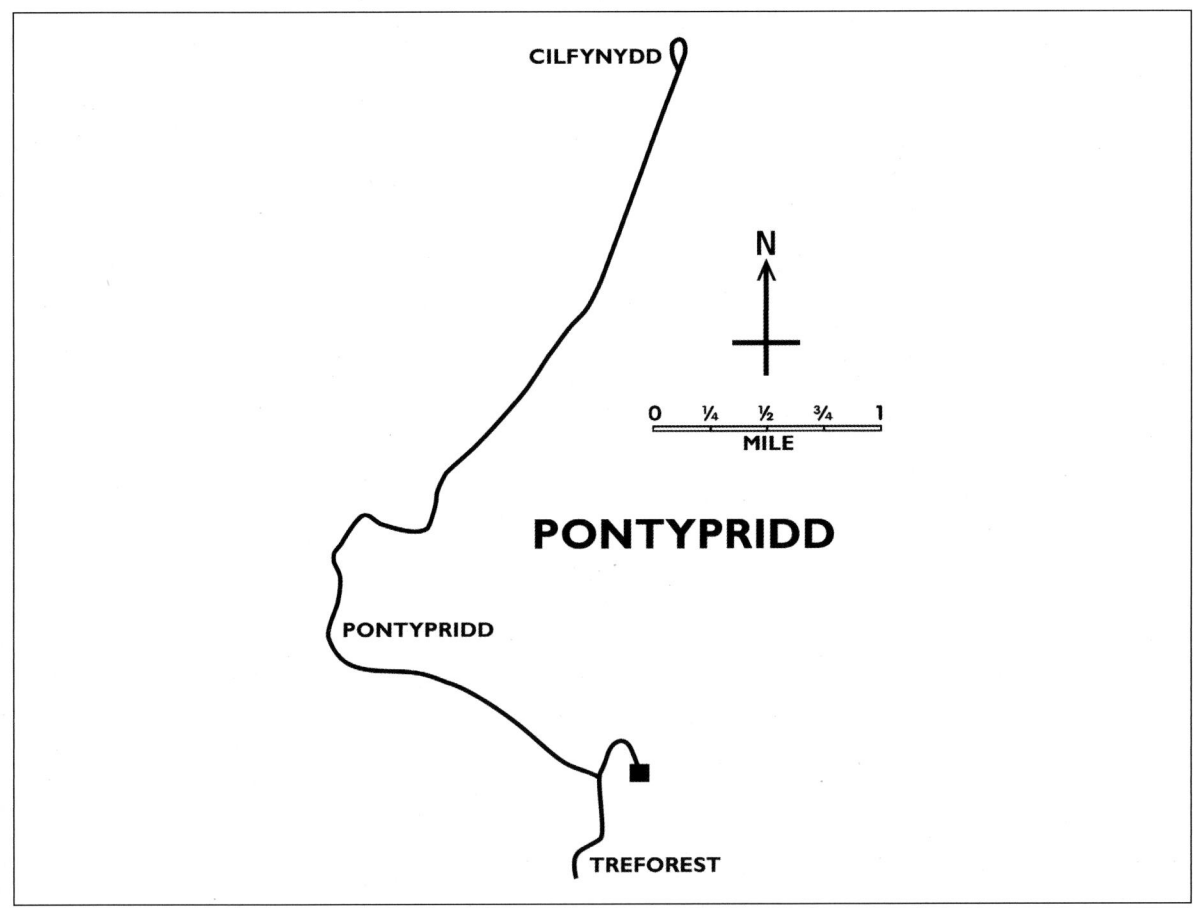

The provision of public transport in the Pontypridd UDC area had its origins in a 3ft 6in gauge horse tramway linking Pontypridd with Porth that opened originally in 1882. One section was eventually become an electric tramway operated by the UDC whilst the remainder became part of the network operated by the Rhondda Tramways Co. The operation of through tram services between Porth and Pontypridd was unique amongst Welsh operators and was to have a direct impact on the development of the UDC's trolleybus network.

Pontypridd's electric trams were inaugurated on 5 March 1905; the system comprised effectively one main route – from Treforest (where the depot was situated) to Cilfynydd – with a second line that ran from Pontypridd itself through to Trehafod, where an end-on connection was made with the tramways of the Rhondda Tramways Co (and over which the through services operated after they were introduced in 1919; they were withdrawn in December 1927 due to disagreements between the two operators).

For the introduction of trolleybus services on 18 September 1930, Pontypridd UDC purchased seven English Electric single-deckers fitted with the same manufacturer's thirty-two-seat bodywork. Pictured in central Pontypridd heading south towards Treforest when virtually brand new is No 3. Evidence of the recently abandoned tramway can still be seen in the road; the track west at this point headed towards Rhondda and a joint tramway service operated between the UDC and the Rhondda Tramways Co. Although the company had considered replacing its trams with trolleybuses, this was not taken further with the result that the section of the UDC tram network towards Rhondda was replaced by buses. Nos 1-7 were sold to Cardiff in 1946 where, as Nos 231-37, they survived in service until withdrawn during 1949 and 1950. *Barry Cross Collection/Online Transport Archive*

By the late 1920s, the UDC's small tramway system was life-expired, and thoughts were turning to its future. Subsidence caused by mining was a problem as was the poor economic climate at the time. In 1929 Pontypridd UDC obtained powers to replace its trams with trolleybuses; however, the Rhondda Tramways Co, which had operated trolleybuses more than a decade earlier, evinced no desire to try that form of transport again and so the trams on the route to Trehafod were replaced by buses.

This left the long route from Treforest to Cilfynydd, a distance of just under 3½ routes miles. The first vehicles – seven English Electric single-deckers – were delivered in 1930. Their arrival allowed for driver training to be introduced alongside the operational trams using a skate along with the tramway overhead and track whilst the overhead was modified for trolleybus operation.

Work on conversion was completed and the new trolleybus service was introduced on 18 September 1930. Initially the trolleybuses operated alongside the trams and buses, but the trams were gradually phased out. The last Pontypridd trams – on the route to Trehafod – operated on 30 August 1931. The possibility of route extensions was examined – but not progressed – in the late 1930s.

The fleet increased by two during the 1930s, but the pressure of wartime traffic saw initially four double-deckers loaned by Hull; when these returned to Humberside, they were replaced by four from Portsmouth. The latter were to remain in South Wales for four years.

During 1945 and 1946, Pontypridd took delivery of eight Karrier Ws fitted with Utility bodywork; their arrival permitted the withdrawal of the original single-deckers from 1930, which were sold to Cardiff Corporation, and the return of the four Portsmouth double-deckers to the South Coast.

As a small operator, Pontypridd was increasingly unviable in the post-war years. The possibility of abandonment was considered – but rejected – in both 1950 and 1954. However, in 1955 the decision was made to convert the route to bus operation with a putative conversion date of 31 October 1956. In the event, the delayed purchase of the replacement buses – allied to the Suez Crisis (which resulted in a number of planned tramway and trolleybus conversions being slightly delayed) – resulted in the closure being delayed (although the trolleybus fleet had already been reduced by two following the sale to Walsall of Nos 14 and 15). The last trolleybuses operated – without ceremony – on 31 January 1957 with the surviving six trolleybuses being sold to South Shields and Doncaster.

On a wet day, with the old bridge across the River Taff in the background, Pontypridd No 11 has just crossed Victoria Bridge heading for Treforest. The old bridge – which is now a Grade I listed structure – was built by William Rodgers and completed in 1756; its newer replacement was completed in 1857. No 11 was one of two Karrier Ws supplied in 1945 that were equipped with Utility bodywork constructed by Weymann. Following withdrawal in 1957, Nos 10 and 11 were sold to Doncaster Corporation. *Marcus Eavis/Online Transport Archive*

Above: **Two further** Karrier Ws were supplied to the UDC during 1945; Nos 12 and 13 were, however, delivered with Utility bodywork manufactured by Park Royal. Here No 12 is seen on Broadway on 11 June 1952. Both were withdrawn in 1957 and were sold to South Shields Corporation (as Nos 238 and 239). *C. Carter/Online Transport Archive*

Opposite above: **A further** quartet of Karrier Ws was delivered to the UDC in 1946. Two – Nos 14 and 15 – were fitted with Roe-built Utility bodywork and No 14 is seen on 11 June 1952, also on Broadway. The delivery of the eight Karriers during 1945 and 1946 permitted the withdrawal of all of the UDC's pre-war single-deckers. Nos 14 and 15 were withdrawn in 1953 and sold to Walsall Corporation. *C. Carter/Online Transport Archive*

Opposite below: **The second** pair of Karrier Ws acquired in 1946 – Nos 8 and 9 – were fitted with Utility bodywork built by Park Royal; here No 8 is pictured on Broadway again on 11 June 1952 with a service heading towards Treforest. Following the conversion of the sole trolleybus route to bus operation on 31 January 1957, Nos 8 and 9 were sold to South Shields Corporation, where they became Nos 236 and 237. *C. Carter/Online Transport Archive*

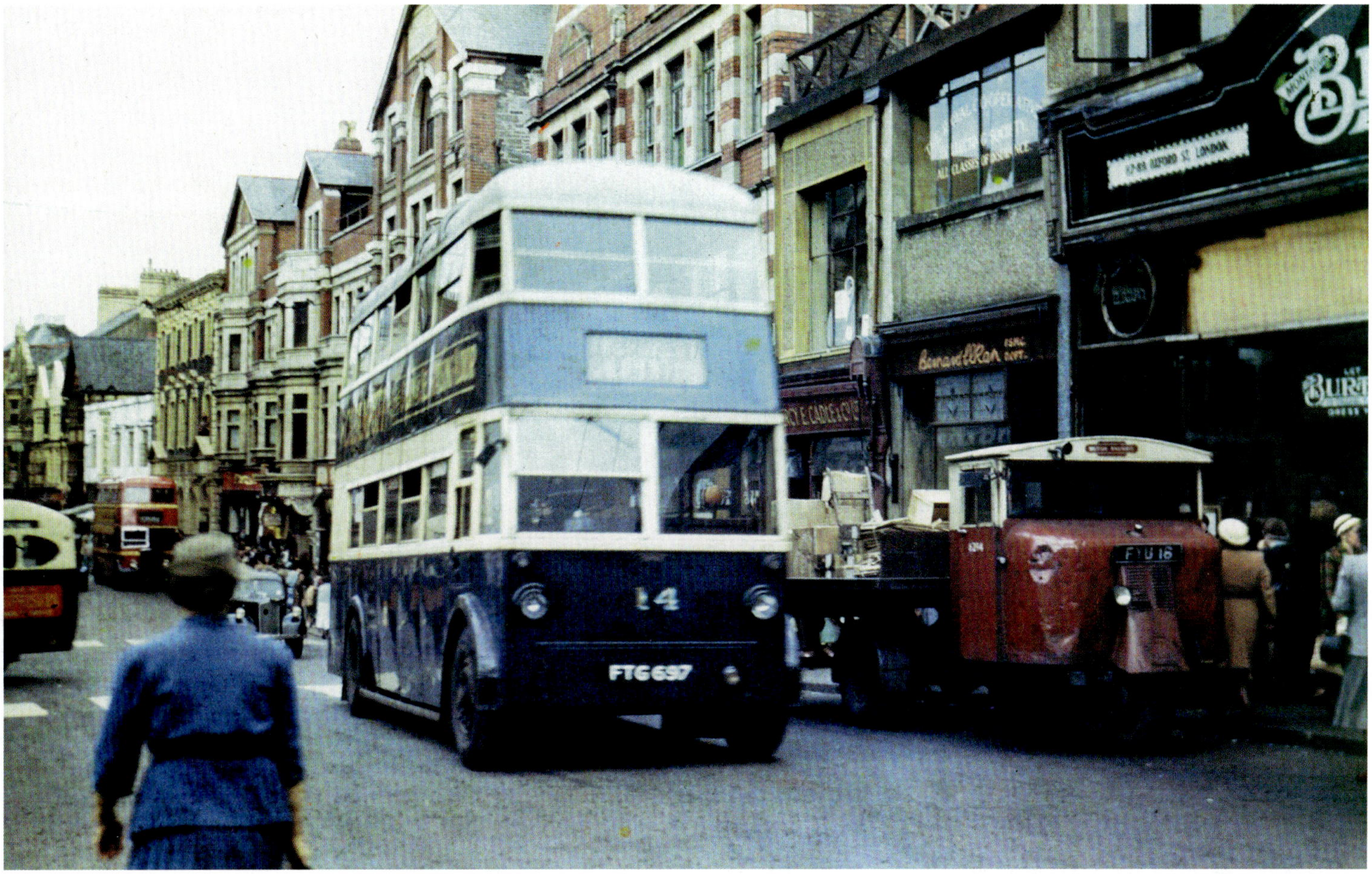
14
FTG 697

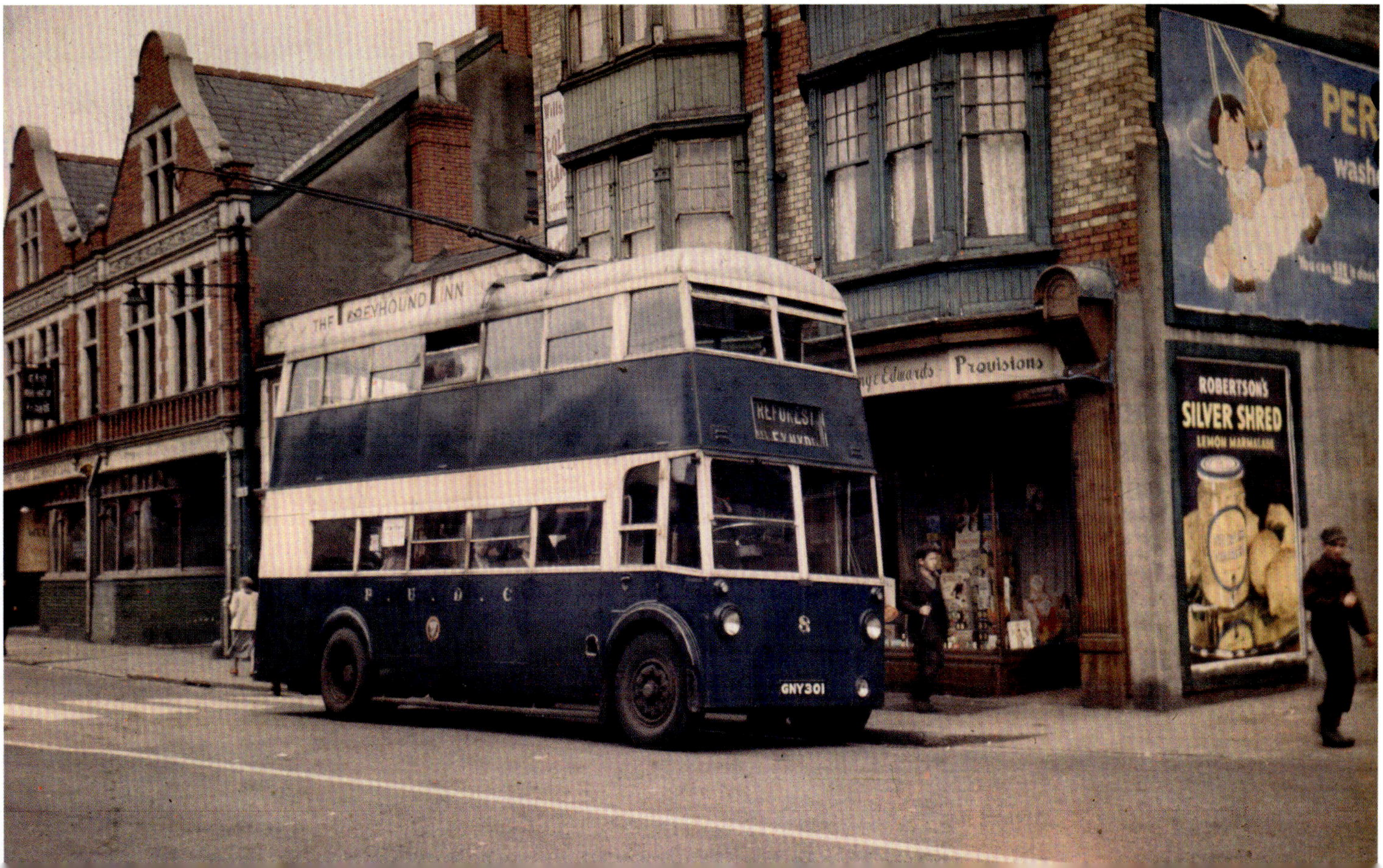
Provisions
P . U . D . C
8
GNY 301
ROBERTSON'S
SILVER SHRED
LEMON MARMALADE

Fleet number	Registration	Chassis	Body	New	Withdrawn	Notes
1-7	TG379/381/383/385/387/389/391	EE SD6WTB	EE B32C	1930	1947	Sold to Cardiff
8	UK8948	Guy BTX	Guy H59R	1930	1946	Guy demonstrator; loaned to Pontypridd December 1930; acquired 1932
9	HY2391	Bristol E	Beadle H60R	1931	1946	Bristol demonstrator; loaned to Pontypridd January 1931; acquired 1932
10 and 11	FNY983-984	Karrier W	Weymann UH56R	1945	1957	Sold to Doncaster
12 and 13	FTG234-235	Karrier W	PR UH56R	1945	1957	Sold to South Shields
8 and 9	GNY301/-302	Karrier W	PR UH56R	1946	1957	Sold to South Shields
14 and 15	FTG697-698	Karrier W	Roe UH56R	1946	1955	Sold to Walsall
Loaned vehicles						
1-4	CRH925-928	Leyland TB4	Weymann H54R	1941	1942	Loaned by Hull Corporation
212-215	RV4658/4659/4662/4663	AEC663T (212)/Sunbeam MS3 (213/14)/AEC 663T (215)	EE H60R (212/13)/MCCW H60R (214/15)	1942	1946	Loaned by Portsmouth Corporation

Route number	From	To	Date Opened	Date Closed	Notes
N/A	Cilfynydd	Treforest	18 September 1930	31 January 1957	

RHONDDA

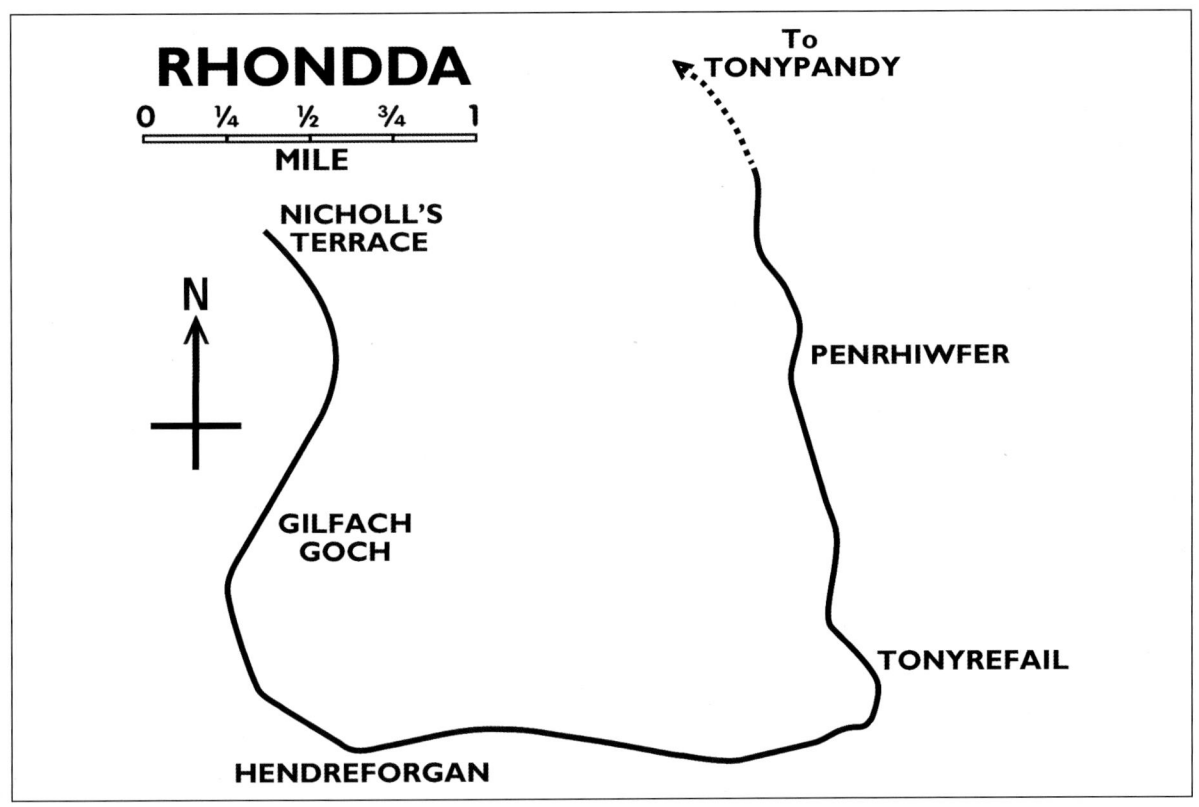

The 3ft 6in gauge tramways in Rhondda were leased by the UDC to the Rhondda Tramways Co, a subsidiary of the National Electric Construction Co. The early years of the twentieth century witnessed the growth of the mining industry in South Wales with a concomitant need to provide transport for those employed in the new collieries.

On 30 March 1912, the company's tramway was opened to Williamstown; the development of this route allied to the opening of new pits in Gilfach Goch during 1911 and 1912, resulted in the neighbouring Llantrisant and Llantwit Fardre Rural District Council obtaining an Act of Parliament in 1912 for the construction of a light railway between the tram terminus at Williamstown and Tonyrefail via Gilfach Goch, a distance of some 4¾ miles. The cost of the line or any extension to the tramway was considered prohibitive and so a cheaper – and more flexible – alternative was sought.

Initially, a motorbus was contemplated but, having visited Rotherham in 1912, the manager and engineer of the Rhondda Tramways Co, H.J. Nisbett, advocated the use of trolleybuses. Having convinced the council, powers to operate trolleybuses were obtained in an Act that received the Royal Assent on 15 August 1913.

In 1914, Brush supplied six single-deck trolleybuses on chassis supplied by Daimler to the Rhondda Tramways Co; however, they were not to remain operational in South Wales for long as, following the abandonment of the service, the six were stored before being sold in 1920, via Clough, Smith & Co to the Teesside Railless Traction Board. As Nos 11-16, the six remained in service with the board until 1926. *Roy Marshall Collection*

The new powers did not, however, cover the overhead installation to be adopted and – following further investigation (by P.E. Stanley, the chief engineer of the National Electric Construction Co) – it was decided to use the Lloyd-Kohler system as subsequently adopted by Stockport. In late 1913, an order was placed with Daimler for six chassis which were to be fitted with single-deck bodies supplied by Brush. However, before the vehicles were completed, the order was amended so that conventional overhead with trolleypoles was adopted. The company intended to use a skate allied to the tram overhead and track in order to access its depot at Troedyrhiw Road in Porth and the Lloyd-Kohler system was incompatible with this.

By the end of 1914, the route was operational; the exact date of operation commencing is uncertain but is generally regarded as 22 December. However, like many other pioneering systems, the Rhondda Tramways Co found that there were major problems in the operation of solid-tyred vehicles on largely unmade roads with the consequent damage to the vehicles.

In early February, following confirmation by Llantrisant and Llantwit Fardre Rural District Council that the road surface would be improved, the company agreed to continue the service; however, in March 1915, No 56 was seriously damaged after running away out of control on one of the many steeply-graded sections of the route.

The consequence of this – as recorded in the local press at the time – was the appearance of notices in the company's tramcar fleet to say that the trolleybus service was suspended; it was never reinstated and was replaced by motorbuses in January 1921. As with the opening date, the exact date of the cessation of services is also unrecorded but certainly occurred during March 1915. The vehicles, however, were not disposed of immediately; they were eventually sold via Clough Smith to the Tees-side Railless Traction Board in 1920.

Fleet number	Registration	Chassis	Body	New	Withdrawn	Notes
55-60	N/A	Daimler	Brush B28	1914	1915	Sold to TRTB via Clough, Smith & Co; the latter purchased them for £2,800 in May 1920 from the Rhondda Tramways Co after five years in store

Route number	From	To	Date Opened	Date Closed	Notes
N/A	Williamstown	Nicholl's Terrace	22 December 1914	March 1915	

WALSALL

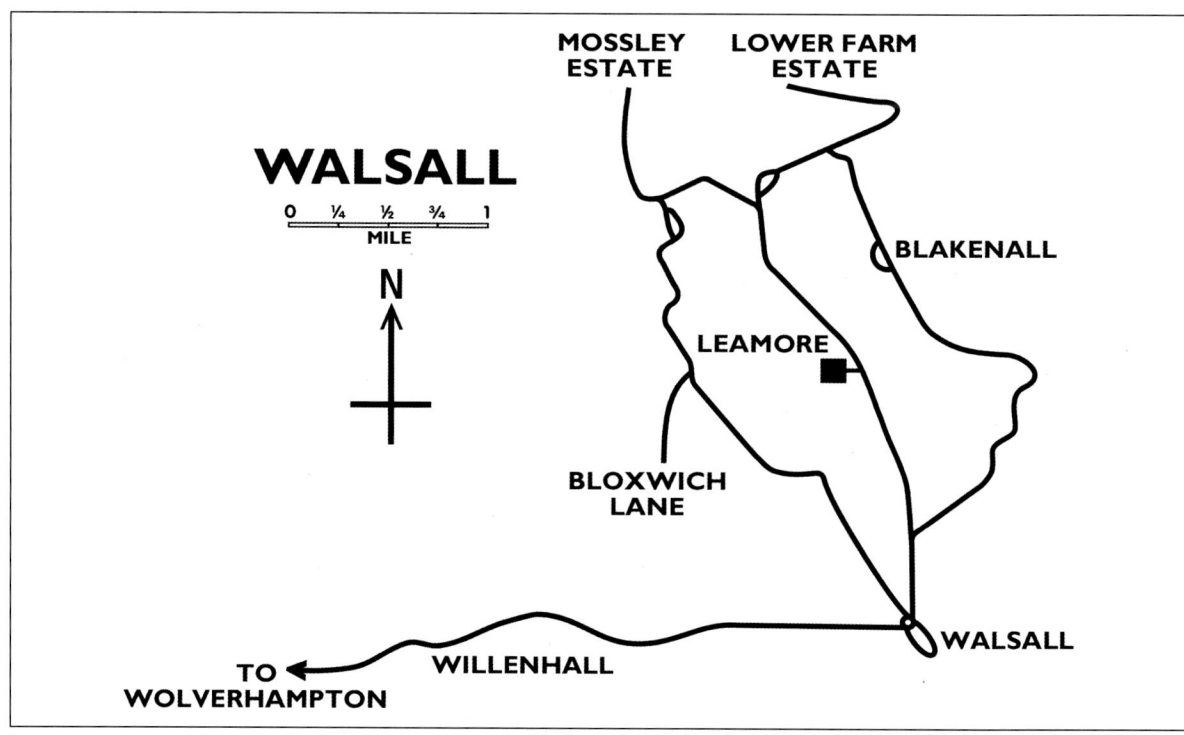

There was a significant network of 3ft 6in gauge tramways serving Birmingham and the Black Country; part of these were acquired by Walsall Corporation from the South Staffordshire Tramways (Lessee) Co Ltd on 1 January 1901 and operated by the corporation from 1 January 1904. The corporation extended the network and, at its peak, operated trams over some 13½ route miles.

Following the opening of the Bradford and Leeds systems in 1911, there was interest in Walsall in adopting the trolleybus to provide feeder services to the tramways and, on 7 August 1914, Royal Assent was given to the Walsall Corporation Act 1914; amongst this Act's provisions were powers to operate trolleybuses. However, nothing further progressed at this stage.

By the mid-1920s, the future of the tramway system was again under consideration although ten new trams had been delivered in 1919 – the last new trams acquired – and the corporation's area of operation had expanded through taking over responsibility for a number of company-operated sections; this process continued through until 1930 when Walsall took over ownership and operation of the once joint services to Wednesbury. On 7 August 1925 Royal Assent was given to the Walsall Corporation Act 1925; this allowed for the replacement of the tram system by trolleybuses as well as for their use on other roads within and beyond the corporation's boundaries. With powers now in place, Walsall initially

For the opening of its first trolleybus service – to Willenhall on 22 July 1931 – Walsall acquired four double-deck trolleybuses; two – Nos 151 and 152 – were AEC 663Ts with English Electric bodywork whilst Nos 153 and 154 were Guy BTXs fitted with bodywork by Brush. Here one of the former is pictured outside the corporation's Birchills depot when new. The two Guys were withdrawn in 1945 with the AECs surviving until the following year. *J. Joyce Collection/Online Transport Archive*

intended to convert the Walsall Wood route; however, this was not progressed and the service was replaced by motorbus on 1 April 1928. All of the early conversions were to motorbus, including the section to Willenhall – converted on 4 February 1929 – where Walsall and Wolverhampton introduced a joint bus service, which supplemented the existing trolleybus service – introduced in May 1927 – between Wolverhampton and Willenhall. Further routes replaced by motorbus included those to Darlaston and Wednesbury on 5 March 1931.

The first trolleybus service to be introduced – on 22 July 1931 – was that to Willenhall; initially the Walsall service terminated at Willenhall with the through service not being introduced until 16 November 1931. In order to access the corporation's depot at Birchills, trolleybus overhead was also erected on the southern section of the Bloxwich tram route.

The success of the new trolleybus service resulted in the conversion of the busy route to Bloxwich; the tramway to Bloxwich had been converted from single track with loops to double track during 1920 and 1921. It was destined to be Walsall's last tram service – on 30 September 1933 – being replaced by a new trolleybus service the following day (this was the date that public service commenced; an official opening had taken place the day before the last tram operated). This introduced passenger services to the section of overhead erected in 1931 for depot workings.

With a fleet of twenty-one – plus four Sunbeams delivered during 1940 – trolleybuses operating two services, this was the extent of the system's development prior to the Second World War, although further powers were enshrined in the Walsall Corporation (Trolley Vehicles) Provisional Order Act 1937, which received the Royal Assent on 5 May 1937. However, as a result of increased traffic during the conflict, the fleet was augmented by the arrival of 12 Sunbeam Ws fitted with Utility bodywork between 1943 and 1946; in addition, two Bournemouth trolleybuses were also loaned between 1943 and 1945. During 1950 and 1951 twelve new Sunbeams were delivered; these and the later Sunbeam Ws allowed for the withdrawal of those trolleybuses delivered in 1931 and the Beadle-bodied Sunbeams of 1933. The surviving early and wartime trolleybuses were all renumbered in 1950. Another change in 1950 was the use of the town centre bus station as a terminus; although this had been used by buses since 1935 (and officially opened on 23 September 1937), it was not accessible by trolleybuses until 1950 following the demolition of property on Stafford Street that permitted the trolleybuses to reach the bus station via St Paul's Street and a loop outside the church.

If there was one pivotal point in the history of the Walsall system, it was the appointment of Ronald Edgley Cox as general manager in June 1952; he had previously been at St Helens. In the history of Britain's trolleybus operators there are a number of individuals whose roles were hugely significant; alongside C.T. Humpidge at Bradford, Edgley Cox was undoubtedly one of these influential figures. Under his management the system grew dramatically and his experimental work on vehicle design – both for the motorbus and for the trolleybus fleets – was dramatic.

On 14 May 1953, Royal Assent was given to the Walsall Corporation (Trolley Vehicles) Provision Order Act 1953; this was followed on 30 July 1954 by Royal Assent

In 1933, Walsall acquired fifteen Sunbeam MS2s in connection with the conversion of the tram route to Bloxwich – completed on 1 October 1933 – with Nos 155-59 being bodied by Beadle, Nos 160-164 by Short and Nos 165-69 by Weymann. Here the last of the Weymann bodied examples – No 169 – is seen when new posed for operation on the through service, route 29, from Wolverhampton to Walsall. In 1950, the fifteen vehicles were renumbered 301-15, but Nos 301-10 were withdrawn by the end of the following year; Nos 311-15 were all withdrawn during 1955 and 1956. *John Meredith Collection/Online Transport Archive*

The last Sunbeam MS2Cs purchased by Walsall was a batch of four – Nos 216-19 – that were new in 1940; fitted with Park Royal sixty-seat bodywork, the four vehicles were to be renumbered 318-21 in 1950. Pictured post-war but still retaining its original number is No 216 heading inbound with a service on route 30. All four were withdrawn in 1956. *Harry Luff/Online Transport Archive*

being granted to the Walsall Corporation Act 1954. The scene was set for the massive extension to the system to cater for the new housing estates being built to the north of the town.

Also in 1953, the corporation took delivery of the first of the pioneering designs that were to be a feature of the trolleybus fleet. This was No 850 – a Sunbeam S7 fitted with a dual-door Willowbrook sixty-two-seat body – that was designed for pay-as-you-enter operation; entrance was via the rear platform – where the conductor was located – and central exit. Never popular, the vehicle was rebuilt in 1961 and was renumbered 350. No 850 was followed by twenty-two Sunbeam F4As with seventy-seat Willowbrook bodywork delivered between 1954 and 1956; their arrival allowed for the withdrawal of older vehicles as well as the planned expansion of the system. These vehicles were the first two-axle 30ft 0in long trolleybuses completed and the first predated the relaxing of the rules and so could only be operated by special dispensation by the Ministry of Transport. Although Cox had plans for an even larger three-axle vehicle, none to this design were completed and Nos 851-72 were to be the last wholly new trolleybuses acquired; thereafter, a number of second-hand vehicles – from Pontypridd, Hastings, Cleethorpes and Ipswich – were purchased, with a number being rebuilt. Another change in 1954 saw the existing depot at Birchills rebuilt.

The first extension since 1933 occurred on 6 June 1955 when trolleybuses replaced motorbuses on the busy service to Blakenall; the larger capacity of the new Sunbeams proved useful for the service. To the west of the Bloxwich route, a new service to the Gypsy Lane Estate (later known as Beechdale) opened on 12 September 1955. This was followed on 10 October 1955 by the extension of the Blakenall route to connect into the existing Bloxwich service; this enabled the completion of the first circular route. The route from Bloxwich to the Mossley Estate was opened in two stages; From Bloxwich to Mossley Estate (Abbey Square) on 3 June 1957 and thence to Mossley Estate (Eagle Hotel) on 30 September 1959. A second circular service was completed on 13 November 1961 by the opening of the section between Gypsy Lane Estate and the Bloxwich to Mossley Estate route. The next extension – on 31 December 1961 – saw the Bloxwich route reach Lower Farm Estate. The final extension was the branch from Stevenson Avenue to Cavendish Road; this opened on 2 September 1963.

The opening to Cavendish Road was, in theory, the start of the creation of a third circular service with plans to extend the route south to connect into the Willenhall route; this, however, was not progressed due to uncertainty as to the route that the M6 – then under construction – was to take. By the time that the motorway was completed, the future of the trolleybus network was much less rosy.

Whilst Walsall was happily investing in its trolleybus network, the reverse was happening in neighbouring Wolverhampton where a policy of conversion had been adopted. Although it had been expected that the through service would survive until

Between 1943 and 1946, Walsall was allocated twelve Sunbeam Ws – Nos 225/26/28-37 – that were fitted with Utility bodywork supplied by Park Royal, Brush or Roe. The first two were Park Royal-bodied and here the second of the duo, by now renumbered 323, is pictured in Walsall ahead of Wolverhampton No 623 – a 1949 Sunbeam F4 also bodied by Park Royal – awaiting departure with a service to Wolverhampton. *W.J. Wyse*

towards the end of the conversion programme, work on the M6 construction brought the date forward, with services between Walsall and Wolverhampton via Willenhall being converted on 31 October 1965.

Like other surviving trolleybus operators, Walsall faced issues with the availability of spares and the ever-increasing cost of electricity allied to the creation of a new central one-way system (in 1967). However, additional powers for the extension of the system were contained within the Walsall Corporation Act 1969, which received the Royal Assent on 22 October 1969, but by that date, the future of the system was no longer in Walsall's control. On 1 October 1969 Walsall's fleet was one of five municipal operations to be subsumed within the new West Midlands PTE. Although Edgley Cox was appointed the new PTE's first director of engineering, the new combined fleet of some 2,500 buses vastly outweighed the fifty-two trolleybuses it inherited. Final conversion was inevitable.

Sunday trolleybus operation had ceased prior to the PTE take-over – on 10 March 1968 – but were to be seen again on 27 December 1969 but this was almost a swan-song. In early 1969 ex-Birmingham motorbuses were transferred to Walsall; this permitted the withdrawal of many of the second-hand trolleybuses in early February and, on 16 February 1970, partial replacement by motorbus would take place. At this stage, the intention was to operate services roughly two-thirds by trolleybus and one-third by motorbus but with the latter being increased as further motorbuses became available. There was some uncertainty during the year as to when the final conversion took place but, by October, there were enough motorbuses to allow for the final withdrawal. The last trolleybuses operated in public service on 2 October 1970. On the following day, four trolleybuses – Nos 342, 353, 859 and 875 – operated a special service for much of the daytime between Walsall bus station and Bloxwich. Following that, three vehicles – Nos 862, 864 and 872 – ran from the depot to the bus station and back. When that was over, Edgley Cox took No 872 out of the entrance to the depot and back in, thus closing the system.

Of the Walsall fleet, two of the second-hand purchases – one ex-Grimsby-Cleethorpes and one ex-Ipswich – survive as do two of the Sunbeam F4As from the mid-1950s – Nos 862 and 872 – and the modified Sunbeam F7 of 1951 – No 342. Sadly, a third F4 – No 864 – was also preserved for some years but was scrapped in 2016.

Recorded on 27 August 1950 – before the renumbering of the fleet – is No 230; this was the third of three Brush-bodied Sunbeam Ws that were new during 1945. All three were withdrawn during 1959. *C. Carter/ Online Transport Archive*

Above: **The twelve** Sunbeam Ws were renumbered Nos 322-33 in 1950 and here numerically the last of the type – No 333 (a Roe-bodied example dating from 1946) – is pictured departing from the bus station with a service to Blakenall. All the Utility-bodied vehicles were withdrawn between 1959 and 1965. *Harry Luff/Online Transport Archive*

Opposite: **During 1950** and 1951, Walsall took delivery of a batch of ten Sunbeam F4s – Nos 344-43 – fitted with Brush fifty-six-seat bodywork; although withdrawal of the type commenced in 1964, five – Nos 338-42 (No 342 had been rebuilt to accommodate sixty-five seated passengers in 1965) – survived to pass into the ownership of West Midlands PTE. All five remained operational when the final services were operated although only No 340 was in service on the final evening. Following withdrawal, No 342 was preserved. One of the earlier casualties – No 337 – is seen here at Blakenall. *Harry Luff/Online Transport Archive*

In 1953, following Edgley Cox's appointment as general manager and with a view towards fleet replacement, Walsall acquired a single Sunbeam S7 with a 62-seat body supplied by Willowbrook. No 850 was designed for pay-as-you-enter operation with a rear entrance and central exit. The doors were controlled by the conductor who sat at a cash desk adjacent to the entrance. However, the vehicle was not popular and was rebuilt in 1961 with a single rear entrance/exit for conventional operation with the seating capacity to sixty-three. It was renumbered 350 at the same time and it is in this guise that the vehicle is pictured here with a service to the Mossley Estate. *Harry Luff/Online Transport Archive*

Above: **In 1954,** fifteen Sunbeam F4As with Willowbrook seventy-seat bodywork were purchased; these were supplemented by an additional seven – Nos 866-72 – two years later and here one of the later batch – No 870 – is seen departing from the bus station on 24 May 1965 with a service on route 15 towards Blakenall. All twenty-two of the type were to remain operational until the final demise of the Walsall system on 2 October 1970 with sixteen being in service that final evening, including No 870, with three others – Nos 862/64/72 – being brought out later for the final obsequies. All three of those that took part in the final tour were subsequently preserved, although – sadly – No 864 was to be scrapped in 2016. *C. Carter/Online Transport Archive*

Right: **Walsall was** another operator to acquire redundant Sunbeam Ws following their withdrawal in Hastings, with eight – ex-Hastings Nos 31, 33, 36-39, 41 and 44 – entering service as Nos 303-10 in 1959. Fitted with Weymann fifty-six-seat bodywork, the last survivors – Nos 304/06-10 – were all withdrawn by the end of February 1970. No 309 is seen here pre-October 1965 awaiting departure from Walsall on the through service to Wolverhampton. *Harry Luff/Online Transport Archive*

Right: **The second** Walsall trolleybus to carry the fleet number 850, seen here at Walsall bus station, was one of two ex-Cleethorpes Crossley TDD42/3s fitted with Roe fifty-four-seat bodywork; it and No 873 both entered service in the West Midlands during 1961 and were to survive until 1970 and 1967 respectively. When withdrawn, No 850 was the last operational Crossley-built trolleybus. *Harry Luff/Online Transport Archive*

Below: **In** addition to the two earlier ex-Cleethorpes vehicles put into service during 1961 – Nos 850 and 873 – Walsall also purchased the four BUT 9611Ts – Nos 59-62 – that had been new originally in 1950. Of these one – No 874 – appeared during 1962 in original condition. Nos 875 and 876 entered service during 1962 and 1963 having been rebuilt by Northern Coach Builders as sixty-nine-seat front-entrance vehicles as shown in this view of No 876 taken at Bloxwich on 1 July 1967. No 877 was similarly rebuilt by Northern Coach Builders but with a slightly smaller seating capacity; Nos 875-77 all survived in to 1970 but only No 875 remained operational on the final day; No 876 last operated on 16 September 1970. *Alan Murray-Rust/Online Transport Archive*

The only one of the quartet of ex-Cleethorpes BUT 9611Ts with Northern Coach Builders bodywork to re-enter service in Walsall in original condition was No 874 (ex-Cleethorpes No 59) which is recorded here on 14 March 1969 on Bloxwich Road, Birchills. Following withdrawal the following year, No 874 was preserved. *Alan Murray-Rust/Online Transport Archive*

The last trolleybuses to be put into service in Walsall were eight Sunbeam F4s with Park Royal bodywork that were acquired second-hand from Ipswich. Nos 344-47/51-54 entered service in the West Midlands and, on 24 May 1965, No 351 is pictured standing at the Walsall terminus of the through route to Wolverhampton. By this date, route 29 was approaching its last few months; it was converted to bus operation at the end of October 1965. The ex-Ipswich vehicles were all withdrawn between 1966 and 1970, with No 347 – ex-Ipswich No 126 – being preserved on withdrawal. *C. Carter/Online Transport Archive*

Fleet number	Registration	Chassis	Body	New	Withdrawn	Notes
151 and 152	DH8311/8312	AEC 663T	EE H60R	1931	1946	
153 and 154	DH8313/8314	Guy BTX	Brush H60R	1931	1945	
155-59 (renumbered 301-04 1950)	ADH1-5	Sunbeam MS2	Beadle H60R	1933	1951	
160-64 (renumbered 305-10 1950)	ADH6-10	Sunbeam MS2	Short H60R	1933	1956	
165-69 (renumbered 311-15 1950)	ADH11-15	Sunbeam MS2	Weymann H60R	1933	1955-56	
187 and 188 (renumbered 316 and 317 1950)	EDH863/864	Sunbeam MS2	PR H60R	1938	1956	
216-19 (renumbered 318-21 1950)	HDH211-214	Sunbeam MS2	PR H60R	1940	1956	
225 and 226 (renumbered 322 and 323 1950)	JDH29/30	Sunbeam W	PR UH56R	1943	1959-61	
228-30 (renumbered 324-26 1950)	JDH331-333	Sunbeam W	Brush UH 56R	1945	1959	
231 and 232 (renumbered 327 and 328 1950)	JDH339/340	Sunbeam W	PR UH56R	1945	1960-61	
233 (renumbered 329 1950)	JDH334	Sunbeam W	Brush UH56R	1945	1965	
234-37 (renumbered 330-33 1950)	JDH430-434	Sunbeam W	Roe UH56R	1946	1965	
334-43	NDH951-060	Sunbeam F4	Brush H56R	1950-51 (342 rebuilt to H65R in 1965)	1964-70	338-43 passed to WMPTE October 1969; 342 preserved
850 (renumbered 350 in 1961)	RDH990	Sunbeam S7	Willowbrook H62D (rebuilt to H63R in 1961)	1953	1967	

Fleet number	Registration	Chassis	Body	New	Withdrawn	Notes
851-72	TDH901-915, XDH66-72	Sunbeam F4A	Willowbrook H70R (866 rebuilt to H71F in 1969 with a view to the introduction of one-man operation)	1954-56	1970	All passed to WMPTE October 1969; 862, 864 and 872 initially preserved; 864 eventually scrapped
301 and 302	FTG697/698	Karrier W	Roe UH56R	1946	1962-63	Ex-Pontypridd 14 and 15; acquired 1956
303-10	BDY806/808/ 811-814/816/ 819	Sunbeam W	Weymann H56R	1948	1970	Ex-Hastings 31, 33, 36-39, 41 and 44; acquired 1959; all bar 305 passed to WMPTE October 1969
850 and 873	HBE541/542	Crossley TDD42/3	Roe H54R	1951	1967-70	Ex-Cleethorpes 63 and 64; acquired 1961; diesel engine experimentally fitted to extended rear platform of 873 in 1968 after withdrawal; 850 was the last active Crossley trolleybus
874-77	GFU692-695	BUT 9611T	NCB H52R (875/76 rebuilt as H69F and 877 as H67F)	1950	1970	Ex-Cleethorpes 59-62; acquired 1962-63
344-47/51-54	ADX193-196/ 189-192	Sunbeam F4	PR H56R	1950	1966-70	All bar 354 passed to WMPTE October 1969; Ex-Ipswich 123-26/19-22; acquired 1962
Wartime loans						
78 and 79	AEL406-407	Sunbeam MS2	PR H56D	1934	1943	Bournemouth 78 and 79; ex-South Shields

Route number	From	To	Date Opened	Date Closed	Notes
28/29	Town Centre	Willenhall	22 July 1931	31 October 1965	Through service (29) to Wolverhampton commenced 16 November 1931
30	Town Centre	Bloxwich	1 October 1933	2 October 1970	Officially opened 29 September but public service only commenced on 1 October
15	Town Centre	Blakenall	6 June 1955	2 October 1970	
33	Town Centre	Gypsy Lane Estate (Beechdale)	12 September 1955	2 October 1970	
15	Blakenall	Bloxwich	10 October 1955	2 October 1970	Created circular route; 15 operated Bus Station-Blakenhall-Bloxwich-Leamore-Bus Station and 30 operated in reverse direction
30 (31 from 31 December 1962)	Bloxwich	Mossley Estate (Abbey Square)	3 June 1957	2 October 1970	
32	Mossley Estate (Abbey Square)	Mossley Estate (Eagle Hotel)	30 September 1959	2 October 1970	
33	Gypsy Lane Estate (Beechdale)	Bloxwich	13 November 1961	2 October 1970	Creation of second circular route Townend Bank-Beechdale Estate-Bloxwich-Leamore-Bus Station
32	Bloxwich	Lower Farm Estate	31 December 1961	2 October 1970	
33	Beechdale (Stevenson Avenue)	Bloxwich Lane (Cavendish Road)	2 September 1963	2 October 1970	

WOLVERHAMPTON

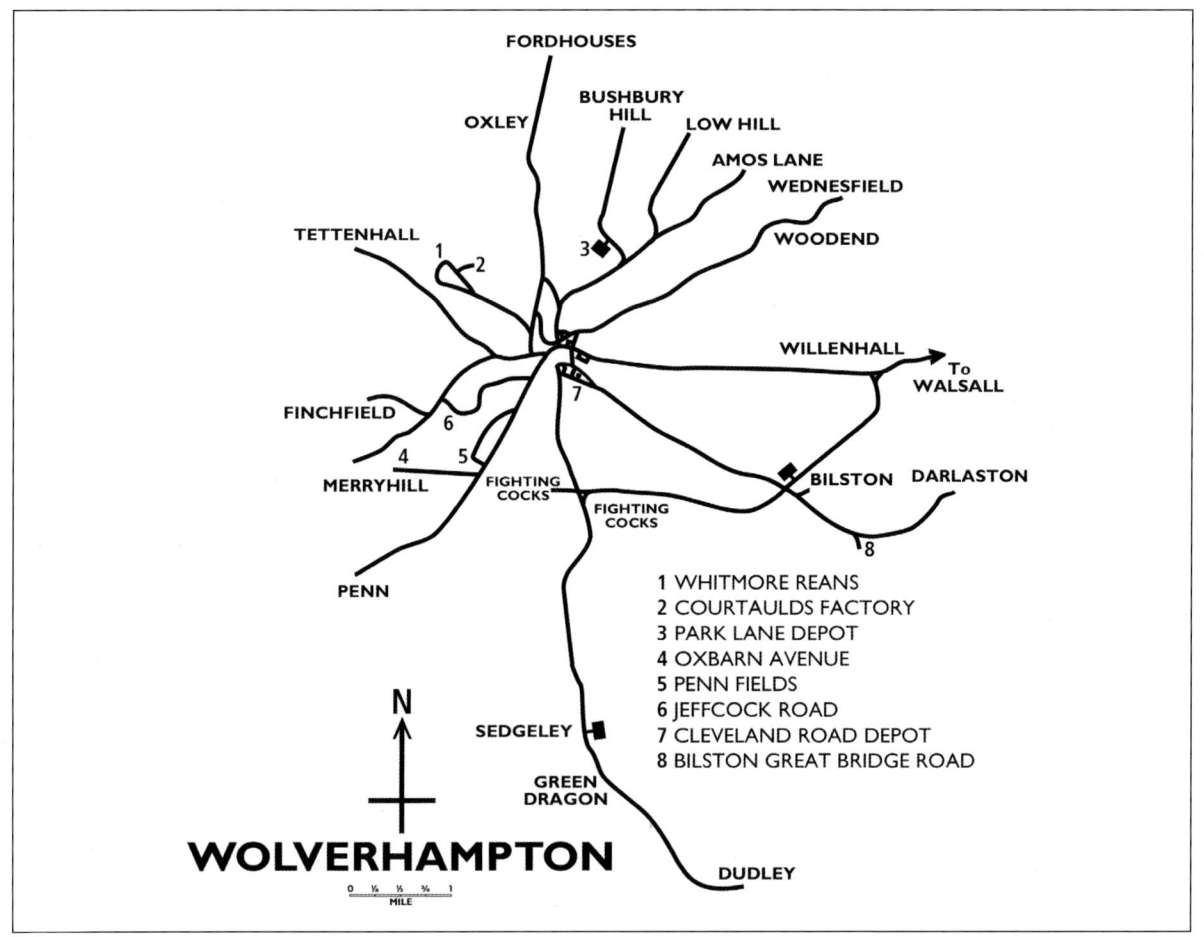

Operating 3ft 6in gauge electric trams from 6 February 1902, having adopted the unusual Lorrain contact stud system initially (subsequently replaced by conventional overhead), Wolverhampton Corporation was in the curious position of abandoning tramways twice. The first occasion – on 26 August 1928 – was the original corporation-owned network; however, having taken over operation of sections of the electric tramways operated by the Wolverhampton District Electric Tramways Ltd in Bilston and Darlaston on 1 September 1928, these routes were last tram operated on 30 November 1928. At the recommendation of the general manager, Charles Owen Silvers, the trolleybus was the preferred means of replacement.

Wolverhampton, in the early 1920s, was looking at the future of its tramway system; a number of routes were predominantly single track with passing loops and it was one of these – the 1¾-mile route to Wednesfield – that was to see the first experimental use

Wolverhampton's first batches of trolleybuses – delivered between 1923 and 1926 – were thirty-two with chassis produced by Tilling Stevens fitted with single-deck bodywork supplied by Dodson. The initial six – Nos 1-6 – were initialled designed to accommodate 40 passengers; this was subsequently reduced to 36, which was the capacity of the remaining twenty-six (Nos 7-32). Pictured is No 26 on route 3A (at the time, this was a unidirectional service that linked Wednesfield with Fordhouses); this entered service in November 1926 and was finally delicensed in May 1937. All of the Tilling Stevens were taken out of service between March 1934 and May 1937. *Barry Cross Collection/ Online Transport Archive*

of trolleybuses as the route was in need of reconstruction. In April 1923, it was agreed to convert the route to trolleybus operation; although Wolverhampton as yet had no powers to operate this type of vehicle, official sanction was given provided that powers were obtained retrospectively; this was achieved through the Wolverhampton Corporation Act 1925, which received the Royal Assent on 7 August 1925. This legislation also paved the way for the corporation's acquisition of the Wolverhampton District's routes in Darlaston, Dudley and Bilston and their conversion to trolleybus operation. The new route – extended to 2¼ miles in length to a new terminus at Pinfold Bridge – commenced operation on 29 October 1923 with the trams having been replaced temporarily on 23 July 1923 by motorbuses for the work of conversion. For the new service six Dodson-bodied Tilling-Stevens TS6s were acquired; these were single-deckers as a result of a low railway bridge.

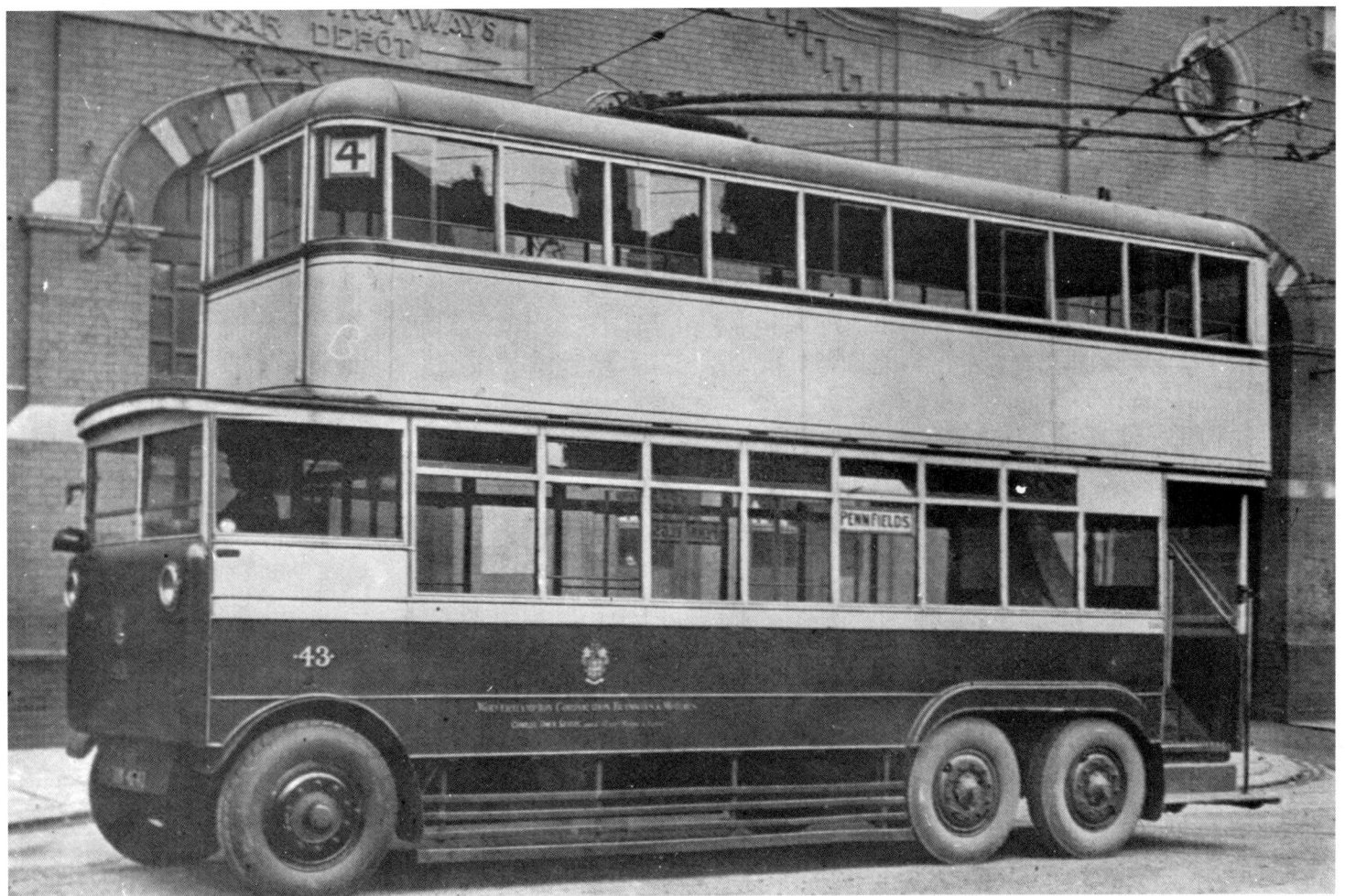

Between 1926 and 1932, Wolverhampton supplemented its fleet through the purchase of locally-produced chassis in the form of 59 Guy BTXs fitted with Dodson bodywork. No 43 pictured here outside Cleveland Road depot was new in 1927 and shows Penn Fields as a destination; this was one of a number of trolleybus routes introduced that year. Although No 43 was a relatively early casualty – it was amongst those of the type withdrawn during 1938 – the last of the type were to remain in service until 1948. Cleveland Road depot, with its distinctive façade, dated originally to 1902 but was extended in 1909, 1913 and 1921; it accommodated tram until August 1928 and was also the corporation's first trolleybus depot. It survived the demise of the trolleybus network and passed to West Midlands PTE in 1969. However, the new owners undertook a major rebuilding – costing more than £1.5 million – which was officially opened on 18 January 1978; the work resulted in the replacement of the frontage. The building closed as a depot on 1 November 1993 and had a number of alternative uses until 2017. Following planning consent, the depot was demolished and the site redeveloped. *Harry Luff Collection/Online Transport Archive*

No 95 entered service in 1933, two years after it was built as the first Sunbeam trolleybus. The MS2 was fitted with a Weymann 61-seat body and had acted as a Sunbeam demonstrator before entering service in Wolverhampton. It was to survive in service until 1948.
Harry Luff Collection/ Online Transport Archive

The new service was a success – it had been transformed from a loss-making into a profitable service – and, in May 1924, it was agreed that the tramway service to Bushbury, which again required renewal, be converted to trolleybus operation and extended, following agreement with Staffordshire County Council, to a new terminus beyond the borough boundary at Fordhouses. Tram operation ceased on 19 August 1924 with the route again being temporarily operated by motorbus to permit conversion; the new trolleybuses were introduced on 9 March 1925. The Fordhouses route was also operated by single-deckers as a result of a low railway bridge; it would not be until 1938 that double-deckers could be used on the service and a further five years before they could be introduced on the route to Wednesfield. This work permitted the withdrawal of the last single-deckers.

The next route to be converted was the long route south to Dudley. This was undertaken in phases. The first stage – from the centre to Fighting Cocks – opened on 26 October 1925; this had been the original corporation tram terminus with the last tram operating on 18 August 1925 to permit conversion. The next section – from Fighting Cocks to Sedgley Bull Ring on 10 November 1925 – saw the trolleybuses operate over a route previously operated by Wolverhampton District for the first time. The service was further extended – the short distance to Sedgley depot – on 11 May 1927 before finally reaching Dudley on 8 July 1927. The new trolleybus terminus was located a short distance beyond the original tram terminus.

Thereafter the system was to grow rapidly. The route to Willenhall opened in two stages: to Neachells Lane on of 15 May 1928 and thence to the Market Place on 16 September 1928. This followed the opening to Penn Fields on 11 July 1928.

During 1934 twenty-six trolleybuses entered service with Wolverhampton; the orders were split almost equally between the two local manufacturers – Guy and Sunbeam (apart from the initial deliveries from Tilling-Stevens and a later Gilford, Wolverhampton acquired all its trolleybus chassis locally). No 205, seen here heading outbound on the Tettenhall route, was a Sunbeam MS3 fitted with Metro-Cammell fifty-eight-seat bodywork. It remained in service until May 1947. *Mervyn Robertson Collection/Online Transport Archive*

No 214 was also a Sunbeam MS3 but this time the fifty-eight-seat bodywork was supplied by Beadle; this was one of a batch of four –Nos 214-17 – that entered service during October and November 1934. All four were withdrawn during 1947 and 1948. *Mervyn Robertson Collection/Online Transport Archive*

Pictured on a route 32 service to Oxbarn Avenue is No 236; this was one of a batch of five – Nos 234-38 – Guy BTs that were fitted with Park Royal fifty-four-seat bodywork and new during 1936. All five were withdrawn during June 1949. *Mervyn Robertson Collection/ Online Transport Archive*

Two further sections opened during 1928 – to Tettenhall on 29 October and to Bilston on 19 November. The latter service was extended to Darlaston on 28 May 1929. The final ex-tramway route – that to Whitmore Reans – which had been operated by motorbuses was converted to trolleybus operation on 27 January 1930; however, instead of connecting into the Tettenhall route, as the trams had historically done, the trolleybuses served a large circular route at the terminus via Court Road and Hordern Road with a new branch serving the Courtaulds factory.

With the conversion of the tramway network completed, the corporation obtained new powers – courtesy of the Wolverhampton Corporation (Trolley Vehicles) Provisional Order Act 1930, which received the Royal Assent on 19 May 1930 – to extend the system. Trolleybuses were introduced to the Bushbury Hill route on 30 November 1931, on 21 March 1932 two services – those to Amos Lane and Pear Tree – commenced operation. On 10 October 1932, the Penn Fields route was extended to Penn via Penn Road; the section of Penn Road avoiding Lea Road and Stubbs Road was also equipped with overhead but the direct route bypassing Penn Fields was not used in passenger traffic until the opening of the Oxbarn Avenue route on 12 February 1934 (this service had previously been operated by motorbuses). The section along Stubbs Road was eventually disconnected with the Penn service running direct along Penn Road from 8 April 1935 and the Penn Fields service terminating at the intersection of Stubbs Road and Lea Road.

The last pre-war deliveries, which entered service during 1938, comprised a total of twenty-three vehicles – Nos 259-81 – of which all bar Nos 264-75 were Guy BTs fitted with either Park Royal or Roe bodywork. Nos 264-75 were Sunbeam MF2s fitted with Park Royal bodywork and here No 267 is seen heading outbound with a service on route 1 towards Tettenhall. All twelve from the batch were withdrawn between October 1949 and January 1950. *Mervyn Robertson Collection/Online Transport Archive*

On 10 April 1933, the route to Bradmore via Great Brickkiln Street, Rayleigh Road and Jeffcock Road was introduced as were the services to Finchfield and Merryhill via Merridale Road; these also a section of the existing overhead on the route to Bradmore west of Jeffcock Road and resulted in the elimination of the Radford terminus with its trolley reverser. Eventually the section along Jeffcock Road was abandoned and a new terminus with trolley reverser established on Downham, Place which served as the terminus of the Jeffcock Road route. On 10 February 1934, the Wednesfield route was extended to Lichfield Road; the final pre-war extension – diverting the Willenhall to Fighting Cocks service from its original terminus at Dudding Road to a new terminus at Goldthorn Hill Road to reduce congestion – was opened on 6 September 1936.

There was to be one further significant change before war was declared in September 1939; this was the opening of the new Park Lane depot on 6 October 1938. This was one of four depots to be used by Wolverhampton's trolleybuses; the other three were the corporation's main depot and works on Cleveland Road and two ex-Wolverhampton District depots in Bilston (from 1928) and Sedgley (from 1930).

To cater for the additional traffic levels experienced during the war twelve vehicles were loaned by Bournemouth Corporation in 1940; these were to remain in Wolverhampton until after the cessation of hostilities in 1945. In 1942 the fleet was further strengthened by the arrival of ten Sunbeam MF2s and, between July 1943 and July 1945, twenty-three Sunbeam Ws. These arrivals permitted the withdrawal of a number of the pre-war vehicles.

On 10 October 1949, Silvers retired as general manager; he had been in post for thirty-four years and had overseen both the conversion programme and the expansion of the network during the 1930s. He was succeeded by his deputy, R.H. Addlesee, who was to be in post for the remainder of the trolleybus era. It has been suggested that he lacked the enthusiasm and vision of his predecessor; certainly, there were few of the dramatic improvements that had been witnessed over the previous twenty-five years. The last new vehicles delivered post-war arrived in 1950; these permitted the withdrawal of most of the surviving pre-war trolleybuses. The only significant change to the fleet thereafter was the programme of rebodying many of the Sunbeam Ws between 1952 and 1962.

There were to be two short extensions opened post-war. The first saw the Wednesfield route extended again to the Albion at Linthouse Lane to serve new housing on 10 January 1955; this was followed on 24 June 1956 by a short extension of the Amos Lane route to the Pheasant again to serve new housing. Additional powers had been granted by the Wolverhampton Corporation (Trolley Vehicles) Provisional Order Act 1955, which received the Royal Assent on 14 May 1955.

By the end of the decade, although there was no immediate threat to the system, there were indications that the future might not be bright. In 1959, Addlesee noted that almost 100 trolleybuses would need to be acquired to replace ageing vehicles; no orders, however, were placed. Two years later, work on the road construction in the centre led to the suspension of all services along Penn Road from 21 January 1961. Although those serving Penn and Penn Fields were reinstated on 21 May 1961, that to Oxbarn Avenue was subsumed into the existing – and parallel – motorbus service to the Warstones Estate and never reintroduced. On 10 March 1961, it was announced that the corporation's

Pictured on Stafford Street on 25 May 1963 is rebodied Sunbeam W No 402; this was one of six of the type delivered during 1944. Unlike the first batch – Nos 296-99 and 400/01 – that were new in 1943 and were fitted with Utility bodywork supplied by Weymann, which were withdrawn unrebodied during 1953, Nos 402-07 had Park Royal Utility bodywork initially and were rebodied by the same supplier during 1952. When seen here, No 402 was approaching the end of its career; it was one of two taken out of service in early June 1963. The remaining four were withdrawn between January 1964 and October 1965. *C. Carter/Online Transport Archive*

policy was now to replace trolleybuses with motorbuses. The first routes to go were those to Penn and Penn Fields on 9 June 1963; these were followed on 30 June 1963 by the service to Tettenhall. The final conversion on 3 November saw trolleybuses eliminated from the routes to Amos Lane, Jeffcock Road, Finchfield, Merryhill, Low Hill and Wednesfield. The following year saw, on 26 January, the conversion of the Fordhouses to Bushbury route and, on 25 October, the service from Willenhall to Fighting Cocks via Bilston.

The first route to succumb during 1965 was that from Whitmore Reans to Bilston and Darlaston on 8 August; this was followed on 31 October by the through service to Walsall. This had been expected to last longer but construction work on the new M6 resulted in its conversion. This left only the services on the long route south to Dudley. These were to survive for almost 18 months before, on 5 March 1967, No 446 operated the last ever passenger service by trolleybus in Wolverhampton. That was the end; there was to be no official ceremony despite more than 40 years' service. Of the Wolverhampton fleet, four examples survive in preservation; these are two of the post-war deliveries, one of the rebodied post-war Sunbeams Ws and a Guy BTX from 1931. The last mentioned is a long-term restoration project at the Black Country Museum.

With two Walsall trolleybuses behind it, Wolverhampton No 413 was one of eleven Sunbeam W4s delivered originally in 1945; of these one – No 408 – was fitted with a Utility 56-seat body supplied by Weymann whilst the remaining ten had similar bodywork supplied by Park Royal. With the exception of No 418, which was rebodied by Roe in 1959, all were rebodied by Park Royal with fifty-four-seat bodywork during 1952 and it is in this rebuilt condition that No 413 is pictured. The eleven vehicles were withdrawn between November 1963 and October 1965; No 413 was one of four that survived to be withdrawn following the conversion of the through service to Walsall at the end of October 1965. *Jim Jordon/Online Transport Archive*

Above: **On 10 July** 1949, No 419 awaits departure from Bilston Street with a service on the route to Dudley. No 419 was the first of a batch of fifteen Sunbeam Ws – Nos 419-33 – that were delivered during 1946 that were fitted with Utility 56-seat bodywork supplied by Park Royal. All were rebodied by Roe during 1958 and 1959, No 419 re-entering service after rebodying during November 1958. No 419 was the first of the batch to be withdrawn – during December 1963 – with the remainder succumbing between October 1965 and March 1967. The last of the batch – No 433 – was preserved after withdrawal in March 1967. *C. Carter/Online Transport Archive*

Opposite above: **Wolverhampton acquired** a further batch of Sunbeam Ws – Nos 434-55 – during 1947. These were equipped with fifty-four-seat bodywork supplied by Park Royal. Typical of the batch is No 449, which is seen here at The Albion (Wednesfield) terminus of route 59 during the summer of 1955. The extension to this terminus had only opened on 10 January 1955; this was destined to be the penultimate extension opened on the system and would only survive until the route was converted to bus operation on 3 November 1963. No 434-55 were all rebodied by Roe between 1960 and 1962; all bar three – Nos 436 withdrawn in 1966, 445 in 1965 and 450 in 1964 – survived into 1967. *Phil Tatt/Online Transport Archive*

Opposite below: **Between 1948** and 1950, Wolverhampton took delivery of 121 new trolleybuses; these were either Sunbeam F4s or Guy BTs but all were fitted with Park Royal fifty-four-seat bodywork that was – as a result of changed Ministry of Transport regulations 8ft 0in wide. The first thirty-six – Nos 456-81 – were Sunbeams and were delivered between September and December 1948. These new vehicles, allied to the subsequent batches, permitted the withdrawal of all the surviving pre-war trolleybuses. Pictured in Walsall on 24 May 1965 is No 465; this was one of six of the batch to survive into 1965 and one of five withdrawn in August that year with the conversion of the routes to Bilston, Darlaston and Whitmore Reans. The last survivor – No 478 – was withdrawn in October 1965, shortly before the conversion of the joint service. *C. Carter/Online Transport Archive*

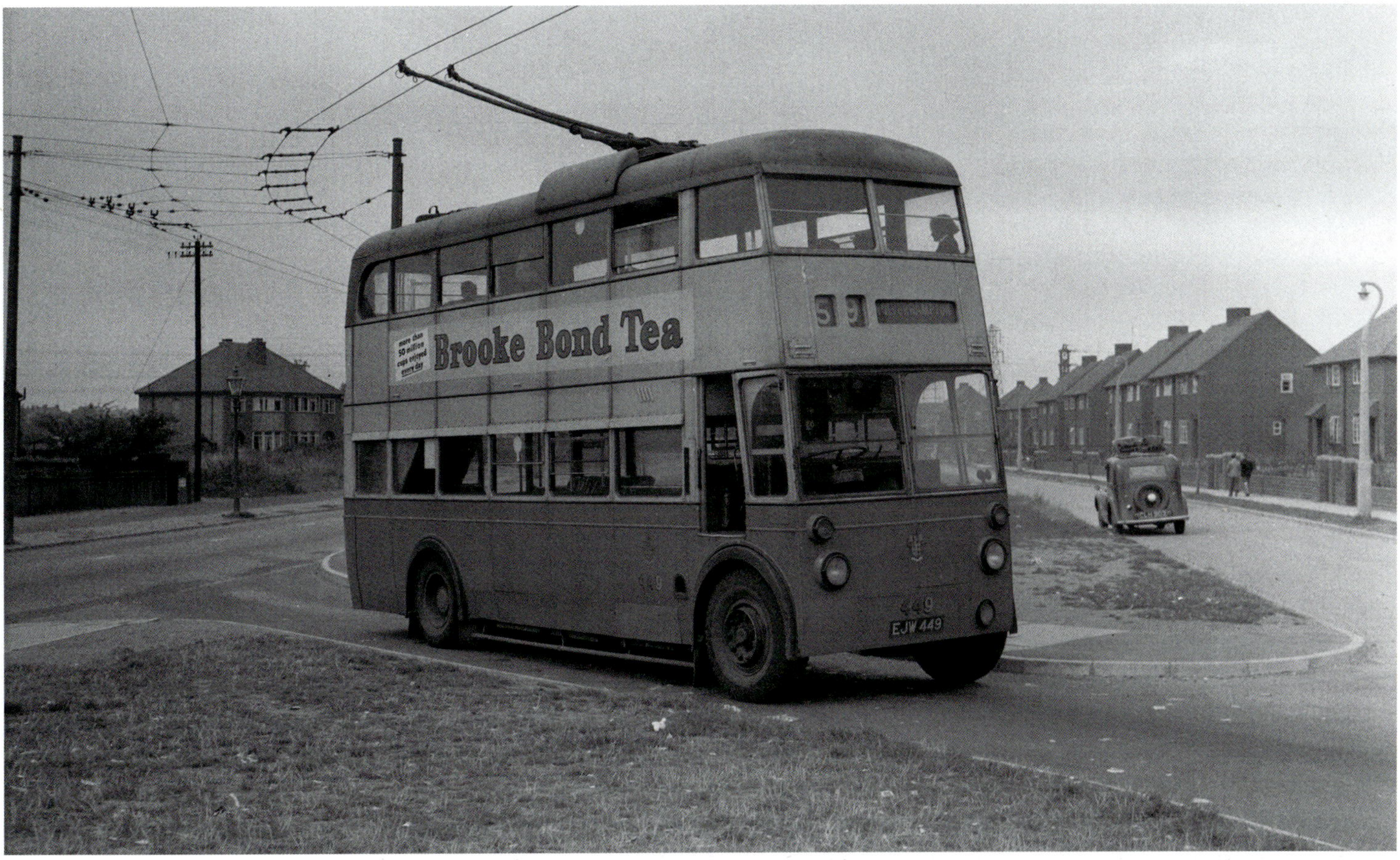
Brooke Bond Tea
EJW 449

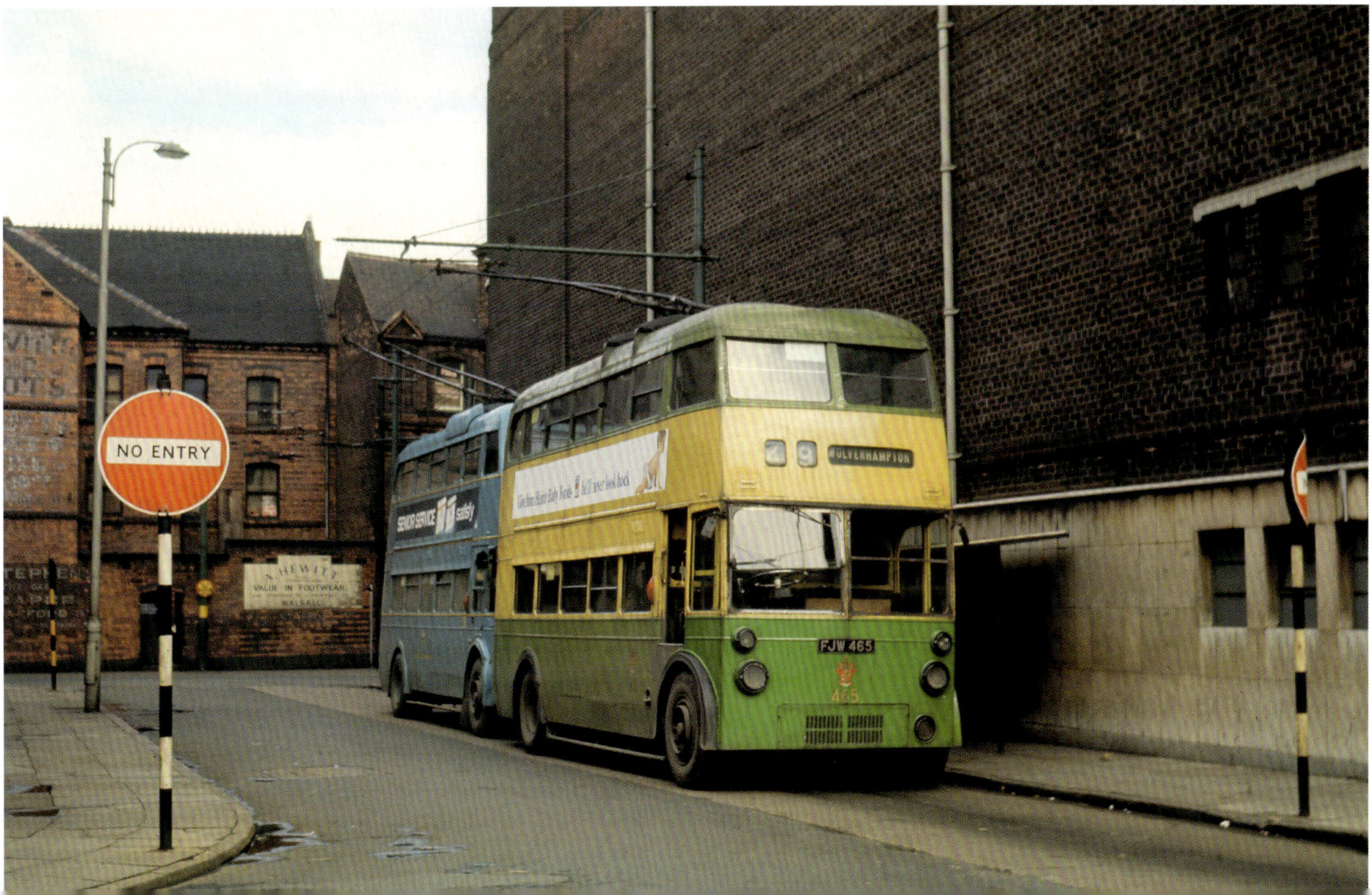
NO ENTRY
WOLVERHAMPTON
FJW 465
SENIOR SERVICE
satisfy

Guy BT No 488 entered service on 17 June 1949 and so was less than a month old when recorded on Lichfield Street on 10 July 1949. This was one of twenty-six of the type – Nos 482-99 and 600-07 – that were delivered between June and October 1949. These were fitted with Park Royal 8ft 0in wide bodies. Although two were withdrawn in 1961 (No 485) and 1962 (No 602), the remainder were withdrawn between June 1963 and August 1965; No 488 was one of the casualties in early November 1963 following the conversion of the routes to Amos Lane, Finchfield, Low Hill and Merry Hill on the third of that month. *C. Carter/Online Transport Archive*

On 13 December 1963, No 626 navigates Garrick Street – part of the large loop that represented the city centre terminus for the route to Dudley – with an outbound service on route 58. Nos 608-30, which were new in 1949, represented the last Sunbeam-badged trolleybuses acquired by Wolverhampton. Fitted with Park Royal fifty-six-seat bodywork, the twenty-three vehicles were all withdrawn between 1961 and 1965; No 626 was one of the last to survive, into August 1965. One of the batch – No 616 – was preserved following withdrawal in late 1963. *Alan Murray-Rust/Online Transport Archive*

Fleet number	Registration	Chassis	Body	New	Withdrawn	Notes
1-6	DA7741-7746	Tilling-Stevens TS6	Dodson B40C (reseated to B36 1927)	1923	1934	
7	DA8814	Tilling-Stevens TS6	Dodson B36C	1924	1934	
8-32	DA9008-9014, UK615-632	Tilling Stevens TS6	Dodson B36C	1925-26	1934-37	
33	UK633	Guy BTX	Dodson H61RO	1926	1936	First Guy trolleybus to be manufactured
34-50	UK634-640/3941/3942/4243-4250	Guy BTX	Dodson H61R	1927	1937-38	
51-56	UK5951-5956	Guy BTX	Dodson H61R	1928	1938	
57-61	UK6357-6361	Guy BTX	Dodson H61R	1929	1938-40	
62-70	UK7962-7966/8767-8770	Guy BYX	Dodson H61R	1930	1943-44	
71-82	UK9971-9978, JW579-582	Guy BTX	Guy H59R	1931	1945-46	78 preserved
83-91	JW983-991	Guy BTX	Dodson H59R	1932	1947-48	
N/A	JW2347	Gilford D	Wycombe H50R	1932	1932	Ex-bus (JD1942) converted to trolleybus; operated November and December 1932
92-94	JW992-994	Sunbeam MS2	Weymann H59R	1933	1947-48	
95	JW526	Sunbeam MS2	Weymann H61R	1931	1948	Ex-demonstrator; first Sunbeam-built trolleybus; acquired 1933
96-98	JW3396-3398	Sunbeam MS3	MC H58R	1934	1946	
99	JW3399	Guy BTX	MC H58R	1934	1946	
200-03	JW3400-3403	Guy BTX	MC H58R	1934	1946-48	
204-05	JW4104-4105	Sunbeam MS3	MC H58R	1934	1945-47	
206-09	JW4106-4109	Sunbeam MF1	PR B32R	1934	1945-49	
210-13	JW4310-4313	Guy BT	PR B32R	1934	1944-45	
214-17	JW4314-4317	Sunbeam MS3	Beadle H58R	1934	1947-48	

Fleet number	Registration	Chassis	Body	New	Withdrawn	Notes
218-21	JW4318-4321	Guy BTX	Beadle H58R	1934-35	1946-49	
222	OC6567	Sunbeam MS2	MC H59R	1934	1949	Ex-demonstrator; Birmingham 67; acquired 1934
223-26	JW7323-7326	Sunbeam MS2	PR H58R	1935	1949	
227-30	JW7327-7330	Guy BTX	Brush H58R	1935	1948-49	
231-33	JW8131-8133	Sunbeam MF1	PR B32R	1936	1944-49	
234-38	JW8134-8138	Guy BT	PR H54R	1936	1949	
239-44	JW8139-8144	Sunbeam MF2	PR H55R	1936	1949	
245	JW8145	Sunbeam MS2	PR H58R	1936	1949	
246-51	AJW46-51	Sunbeam MF2	Beadle H54R	1937	1949	
252-58	AJW52-57, BDA358	Guy BT	Beadle H54R	1937	1949	
259-63	BDA359-363	Guy BT	Roe H54R	1938	1949-50	
264-75	BDA364-369, BJW170-175	Sunbeam MF2	PR H54R	1938	1949-50	
276-81	BJW176-181	Guy BT	PR H54R	1938	1949-53	
282-83	DDA182-183	Sunbeam MF2	PR H54R	1940	1950-52	282 sold to Belfast (235)
284-85	DDA184-185	Sunbeam MF2	Roe H54R	1940	1950	
286-90	DDA986-990	Sunbeam MF2	PR H54R	1942	1952	All sold to Belfast (236-40)
291-95	DDA991-995	Sunbeam MF2	Roe H54R	1942	1952	All sold to Belfast (241-45)
296-99, 400-01	DJW596-601	Sunbeam W	Weymann UH56R	1943	1953	
402-07	DJW902-907	Sunbeam W	PR UH56R (rebodied by PR to H54R in 1952)	1944	1963-65	
408	DJW938	Sunbeam W	Weymann UH56R (rebodied by PR to H54R in 1952)	1945	1965	
409-13	DJW939-943	Sunbeam W	PR UH56R (rebodied by PR to H54R in 1952)	1945	1963-65	

Fleet number	Registration	Chassis	Body	New	Withdrawn	Notes
414-18	DUK14-18	Sunbeam W	Park Royal UH56R (414-17 rebodied by PR to H54R in 1952; 418 rebodied by Roe to H60R in 1959)	1945	1963-65	
419-33	DUK41/820-833	Sunbeam W	PR UH56R (rebodied to H60R by Roe in 1958-59)	1946	1964-67	433 preserved
434-55	EJW434-455	Sunbeam W	PR H54R (rebodied to H60R by Roe 1960-62)	1948	1964-67	
456-81	FJW456-481	Sunbeam F4	PR H54R	1948	1961-65	
482-99, 600-07	FJW482-499/600-607	Guy BT	PR H54R	1949	1961-65	
608-30	FJW608-630	Sunbeam F4	PR H54R	1949-50	1961-65	616 preserved
631-44	FJW631-644	Guy BT	PR H54R	1949	1963-65	
645-54	FJW631-654	Guy BT	PR H54R	1950	1961-67	654 preserved
Wartime loans						
105 and 107	ALJ979/981	Sunbeam MS2	PR H56D	1935	1946	Bournemouth 105 and 107; loaned from 1940
129-32/37	BEL814-817/822	Sunbeam MS2	PR H56D	1935	1946-48	Bournemouth 129-32/37; loaned from 1940
156/61/68	BRU7/12/19	Sunbeam MS2	PR H56D	1935-36	1946-48	Bournemouth 156/61/68; loaned from 1940
176	AEL404	Sunbeam MS2	PR H56D	1934	1948	Bournemouth 76; renumbered in Wolverhampton; loaned from 1940
184	ALJ60	Sunbeam MS2	PR H56D	1934	1946	Bournemouth 84; renumbered in Wolverhampton; loaned from 1940

Route number	From	To	Date Opened	Date Closed	Notes
6	Broad Street	Wednesfield (Penfold Bridge)	29 October 1923	3 November 1963	
3A/6/6A (later 3)	Broad Street	Fordhouses	9 March 1925	26 January 1964	Initially linked to Wednesfield as cross town routes with 3 (short working to Bushbury) and 3A westbound services and 6 (peak hour only and 6A) being eastbound; subsequently linked to Bushbury Hill for cross-town service from 10 May 1937 with short working at Oxley (Church Road)
8	Snow Hill	Fighting Cocks	26 October 1925	5 March 1967	
8A (later route 61)	Fighting Cocks	Sedgley Bull Ring	10 November 1925	5 March 1967	
4	Victoria Square	Penn Fields	11 July 1927	9 June 1963	Suspended 22 January to 21 May 1961 due to roadworks
5	Queen Street (later St James's Square)	Willenhall (Neachells Lane)	15 May 1927	31 October 1965	
8B	Sedgley Bull Ring	Sedgley Depot	11 May 1927	5 March 1967	Temporary terminus until opening through to Dudley
8B (later route 58)	Sedgley Depot	Dudley	8 July 1927	5 March 1967	Route number 58 also used for short working to Green Dragon
5	Willenhall (Neachells Lane)	Willenhall (Market Place)	16 September 1927	31 October 1965	Through service (initially route 5A later route 29) to Walsall introduced 16 November 1931
1	Victoria Square	Tettenhall	29 October 1927	30 June 1963	
2/7	Victoria Square	Bilston	19 November 1928	8 August 1965	
2A/7A (later 2 and 7)	Bilston	Darlaston	27 May 1929	8 August 1965	
2/2A/7/7A (later 2 and 7)	Victoria Square	Whitmore Reans	27 January 1930	8 August 1965	Linked to Bilston and Darlaston services 2/2A operated westbound and 7/7A eastbound; 2A and 7A operated anticlockwise around the Whitmore Reans loop and 2 and 7 operated clockwise
N/A	Hordern Road	Courtaulds factory	27 January 1930	October 1949	Spur off the Whitmore Reans circular route

Route number	From	To	Date Opened	Date Closed	Notes
25	Willenhall	Fighting Cocks (via Bilston)	27 October 1930	25 October 1964	24 was for a period a short working from Willenhall to Bilston; route finally converted due to rebuilding work on railway bridge at Willenhall
9A	Broad Street	Bushbury Hill	30 November 1931	26 January 1964	Linked to Fordhouses for cross-town service from 10 May 1937
11A (later 11)	Penn Fields	Penn	10 October 1932	9 June 1963	Route 11 was short working to Mount Road; section along Stubbs Road from Penn Fields to Penn Road closed following opening of route 11 in 1935 and introduction of services to the existing overhead along Penn Road; suspended 22 January to 21 May 1961 due to roadworks
9B/13 (later 13 only)	Low Hill (Pear Tree)	Merry Hill	10 April 1933	3 November 1963	Cross-town service with 9B operating eastbound and 13 westbound
9B/12A (later 12 only)	Low Hill (Pear Tree)	Finchfield	10 April 1933	3 November 1963	Cross-town service with 9B operating eastbound and 12A westbound
9/12	Amos Lane	Bradmore (via Brickkiln Street Jeffcock Road)	10 April 1933	3 November 1963	Cross-town service where route 9 operated eastbound and route 12 westbound; cut back to Jeffcock Road – later route 9– after opening of Finchfield and Merryhill services; suspended 22 January to 21 May 1961 due to roadworks
6	Wednesfield (Penfold Bridge)	Wednesfield (Wood End)	10 February 1934	3 November 1963	
32	Chubb Street	Oxbarn Avenue	12 February 1934	22 January 1961	Originally suspended but never reinstated due to roadworks
11	Railway Street	Penn (via Penn Road)	8 April 1935	9 June 1963	Suspended 22 January to 21 May 1961 due to roadworks
25	Fighting Cocks (Dudding Road)	Fighting Cocks (Goldthorn Hill Road)	6 September 1936	25 October 1964	Relocation of terminus from Dudley Road via new section to junction of Ward Road and Goldthorn Hill Road
47		Bilston (Great Bridge Road)	24 October 1949	8 August 1965	Short spur and loop opened off Moxley Road
59	Wednesfield (Wood End)	Wednesfield (The Albion)	10 January 1955	3 November 1963	
9 (88 from 29 September 1963)	Amos Lane	Pheasant Inn (Lower Prestwood Road)	24 June 1956	3 November 1963	Route renumbered following conversion of Jeffcock Road section

BIBLIOGRAPHY

Barker, Colin, et al; *Trolleybus Classics* series; Middleton Press; 1995 onwards
Blacker, Ken; *The London Trolleybus – Volume 1: 1931-1945*; Capital Transport; 2002
Bowen, D.G., and Callow, J.; *The Cardiff Trolleybus*; NTA; 1970
Buses Illustrated/Buses; Ian Allan Ltd; since 1949
Canneaux, T.P, and Hanson, N.H.; *The Trolleybuses of Newcastle upon Tyne 1936-1966 (Second Edition)*; Newcastle upon Tyne City Libraries; 1985
Challoner, Eric; *Trolleybus Days in Wolverhampton*; LRTA / Trolleybooks; 2017
Griffiths, Geoff; *Llanelly Trolleybuses*; Trolleybooks; 1992
Hall, D.A.; *Reading Trolleybuses*; Trolleybooks; 1991
Joyce, J., King, J. S. and Newman, A.G.; *British Trolleybus Systems*; Ian Allan Ltd; 1986
Joyce, J.; *Trolleybus Trails*; Ian Allan Ltd; 1963
King, J.S.; *Keighley Corporation Transport*; Advertiser Press; 1964
Kraemer-John, Glyn, and Bishop, John; *Trolleybus Memories: Brighton*; Ian Allan Publishing; 2007
Kraemer-Johnson, Glyn, and Bishop, John; *Trolleybus Memories: Brighton*; Ian Allan Publishing; 2007
Lockwood, Stephen; *A-Z of British Trolleybuses*; The Crowood Press; 2017
Lumb, Geoff; *Ian Allan Transport Library: British Trolleybuses 1911-1972*; Ian Allan Ltd; 1995
Mayou, Archie, Barker, Terry, and Stanford, John; *Birmingham Corporation Tramways: Trams and Trolleybuses*; Transport Publishing Co; 1982
Neale, R.F.A. (Ed); *London's Trolleybuses: A Fleet History*; PSV Circle / Omnibus Society; undated
Owen, Nicholas; *History of the British Trolleybus*; David & Charles; 1974
Potter, D. F., Webb, J. S. and Wilson, Ray; *Walsall Corporation Transport*; Birmingham Transport Historical Group; 1981
Scotney, D.J.S.; *The Maidstone Trolleybus*; NTA; 1972
Symons, R.D.H., and Creswell, P.R.; *British Trolleybuses*; Ian Allan Ltd; 1967
Taylor, Hugh; *London Trolleybus Routes*; Capital Transport; 1994
Taylor, Hugh; *London Trolleybuses: A Class Album*; Capital Transport; 2006
Trolleybus Magazine; National Trolleybus Association
Turner, Keith, Smith, Paul and Smith, Shirley; *The Directory of British Tram Depots*; OPC; 2001
Walsall's Trolleybuses; West Midlands PTE; 1970
Webber, Mick; *London Trolleybus Chronology*; Ian Allan Publishing; 1997